Praise for *The Boy Who Really, Really Wanted to Have Sex*

"John McNally's childhood was the perfect setup for a writer: fat, lonely, poor, reckless, seldom supervised, and filled with the power of his imagination. He writes with warmth and humor about his early years, and not a trace of self-pity or blame. Come for the story but stay for the prose. The book's structure is remarkable and innovative. John McNally has the rare skill of making difficult work look easy. This book will become a classic of memoir."
—Chris Offutt, author of *My Father, the Pornographer* and *Kentucky Straight*

"John McNally's effortlessly funny, marvelously crafted fiction is a joy and an inspiration. Now, with *The Boy Who Really, Really Wanted To Have Sex*, McNally has produced a vivid memoir of growing up in the seventies that might be his best work yet. The consideration he has given to his childhood experiences, to his family history, to his faults and his fascinations, is quick-witted and unsparing." —Owen King, author of *Double Feature* and co-author of *Sleeping Beauties*

"John McNally's funny and heart-clenchingly sincere new memoir is such a familiar heartbreak that at times I had to set the book down and remedy my own past against it. The achy yearnings of a child who knows more than he understands create a series of sorrowful longings, misplaced and misunderstood by nearly everyone around him, including McNally himself. Yes, there are shapely women, and young pretty girls who fill the space of fantasy and cravings, but McNally ultimately discovers how mysteries of the flesh and heart, once solved, can never truly satisfy the urge from whence they came." —Deborah Reed, author of *The Days When Birds Come Back*

"John McNally's work has always left me on a teeter-totter of sorts: laughing out loud one moment, wincing the next. *The Boy Who Really, Really Wanted To Have Sex* is no exception. We find discombobulated parents, girls who remain out of reach, a body that seems full of practical jokes, and pals who laugh at them: the trappings of a typical coming of age story. Yet in McNally's hands, these mortifying years turn anything but typical. This is a horror story recounted by the finest of jesters in the court of the seventies and eighties which McNally delivers in the stunned and astute voice of a boy who just wants ... well you know what he wants." —Bruce Holbert, author of *The Hour of Lead* and *Lonesome Animals*

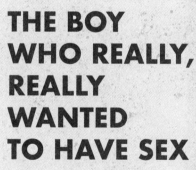

THE BOY
WHO REALLY,
REALLY
WANTED
TO HAVE SEX

THE MEMOIR OF A FAT KID

JOHN McNALLY

ELEPHANT
ROCK
BOOKS

Ashford : Connecticut
elephantrockbooks.com

ISBN: 978-0-9968649-5-4

Library of Congress Control Number: 2017951093

Printed in the United States of America

Book Design by Amanda Schwarz,
Fisheye Graphic Services, Chicago

First Edition
10 9 8 7 6 5 4 3 2 1

Elephant Rock Books
Ashford, Connecticut
elephantrockbooks.com

For my good friend
Eric G. Wilson

Whether I shall turn out to be the hero of my own life, or whether that station will be held by anybody else, these pages must show.

—Charles Dickens, *David Copperfield*

Please allow me to introduce myself…

—Mick Jagger, "Sympathy for the Devil"

Other books by John McNally

Lord of the Ralphs, 2015

Vivid and Continuous: Essays and Exercises for Writing Fiction, 2013

After the Workshop, 2010

The Creative Writer's Survival Guide: Advice from an Unrepentant Novelist, 2010

Ghosts of Chicago, 2008

America's Report Card, 2006

The Book of Ralph, 2004

Troublemakers, 2000

TABLE OF CONTENTS

PROLOGUE: PICTURE DAY

My grade school photos tell the story.

In kindergarten, my hair is thick and parted on the side; it has been recently cut by a professional—i.e., the corner barber. My expression, however, is that of someone much older—a man who's been told by his accountant that he just lost everything in the stock market. I am in my last two years of being thin, but I don't appreciate this fact since I am just a boy and not a soothsayer.

In first grade, a lock of hair has twisted onto my forehead like Superman's, but my eyes are bloodshot and my shirt is stained from where I've been weeping. I'm in a new school in a new city, and I have been reprimanded by every teacher I encounter for not knowing where I should be. Thus begins my hatred for authority figures.

In second grade, my hair is crooked, cut that very morning by my mother. I've put on a few pounds since my weeping photo. My vest, which looks like something a plump Frankenstein might have worn in one of the later Universal sequels, is too tight. I'm trying to smile, but I'm clearly disturbed by my new appearance.

In third grade, my hair is slicked to the side and behind my ears—slicked with what, I do not know. I'm wearing wire-framed glasses and look as though I might have been the very accountant who informed my kindergarten self that he had lost it all. Furthermore, I look pleased to have delivered the news.

In fourth grade, I've gained a preposterous amount of weight, and my long hair curls out in every possible direction. Despite what I'm wearing—a polyester turtleneck / plaid-sweater one-piece that is more tablecloth than shirt—I'm smiling more than I have in my previous photos; my eyes are gleaming. If I wasn't nine years old, you'd think I was enjoying the first day of a bender.

In fifth grade, I've returned to looking somber, no smile, but it's clear I'm amused by the situation I'm in. This is the fifth school I've attended in five years, and I'm starting to learn irony. My hair, flat once again, has more bulk than ever before.

In sixth grade, I have no control over my hair. It juts out at odd directions, and the beauty school trainee who did the job cut my bangs too short. I'm missing two upper teeth and wearing a puka shell necklace. I'm laughing—God only knows why.

In seventh grade, I'm fatter than I've ever been. Whatever problems my hair is having is a moot point next to my weight. My future as a security guard is looking frighteningly more promising. (Oh yeah. One more thing. I appear to be growing breasts. *That's* how much weight I've gained.)

In eighth grade, my hair is a sculpture—thick and wavy—kept in place with a can's worth of Aqua Net. If someone were to come near me with a cigarette, I'd go up in flames. My prescription glasses have tinted lenses. The good news is, I'm starting to slim down, and the blue leisure suit is looking pretty sweet on me.

And so it goes. Fat one year, not quite as fat the next. Hair parted, hair feathered, hair crooked, hair left to its own volition. In grade school, I was a lycanthrope that could never quite make the final transformation from man to beast. My body would get a stage or two into the metamorphosis and then pause before returning to some previous incarnation, or, rather, some new, mutated version of my original self.

But then came high school. Something profound happened. I became cool—or, perhaps more accurately, the *potential* for cool descended upon me. It didn't happen overnight, but it felt as though it had: one year, I was a 210-pound, five-foot-four seventh grader; two years later, I was a 125-pound, five-foot-eleven (and still growing) freshman at Reavis High School. I was, for all practical purposes, a different person. Girls not only liked me, they pursued me! Not the girls who had known me as a smart-ass fatso; those girls didn't know what the hell to make of me and therefore kept their distance. To them, I was probably a genetic mutant, a freak show attraction, as appalling as naked conjoined twins doing cartwheels across a splintery stage. But those other girls—girls I would have pined for in grade school, girls who didn't know the fat me—began flirting with me. They sometimes whispered startling things in my ear. It was every fat boy's dream, and I should have wallowed in it.

My life, I realize now, could have been a scene right out of Robert Guccione's *Caligula*. It was 1979, the tail end of the sexual revolution—before herpes, before AIDS. No one was afraid of sex. Even Jimmy Carter had confessed to *Playboy* that he had lust in his heart—a quote taken out of context and exploited, but still . . . Lust! I understood! True, I was only thirteen years old, and I would have been happy with a serious make-out session in the backseat of an older girl's Nova, but my mind often ran rampant with more erotic (and unlikely) scenarios. Sex on a roller coaster. Sex at a Meat Loaf concert. For all practical purposes I should have been cool, but there was a problem: I had been uncool for so long that I had no idea how to handle the transformation. I was like the guy who lives in a school bus until he wins the lotto. We all know this story. This guy, the lotto winner, doesn't know how to handle his newfound wealth, and so he goes a little crazy, indulging every possible vice while annoying everyone who comes into contact with him. I was the fat-to-skinny version of his rags to riches. I know now that being cool has more to do with attitude than looks, but this was lost on me at thirteen. In truth, I was cooler as a fat, ironic kid who made snide comments about teachers during class than I was as a skinny kid who wasn't sure how to respond to girls.

It's not easy to admit, but I had all kinds of built-up anger, too, and it came out in fits and starts.

When Juan Gonzalez, a classmate from one of my many former grade schools, came up to me during lunch and said, "You used to be fat, didn't you?" I pulled the straw from my milkshake and quickly flicked it at him. A glob of shake hit Juan square in the face. He screamed as though I'd flung battery acid at him, and then he took off running, never to speak to me again.

I'm not proud of what I became: an angry fat kid inside the body of a skinny kid. Eventually, the anger dissipated. But I remained as shy around girls as the fat me had been. Around certain girls, at least. Girls I had wanted to date but couldn't get the nerve to ask out.

Take Sara. She was in my dramatic arts class sophomore year, and I couldn't help myself: I stared at her. She was big boned in a way that was not a euphemism for being overweight. At sixteen, she had already bloomed into full womanhood, and she carried herself with confidence: an adult among children. While other girls got perms that didn't compliment the size of their heads or that made them look like toy poodles, Sara was living, breathing proof that a perm could not only work but could be damn sexy as well. She was also one of the very few girls in my school to understand the knee-weakening power of cleavage. I developed a kind of apnea that year, taking quick, unexpected breaths each time I saw her in a low-cut blouse, that spillage of flesh and temptation. Her cleavage made me feel the way Pentecostals must feel when they begin speaking in tongues. One day in the library, I caught sight of Sara's cleavage. I recognized whose it was and, without looking up take in the whole of her, savored it. Sara was leaning on the counter, waiting for help, and I was around the counter's corner, staring. When I finally did peek up, Sara was already looking into my eyes and smiling. She had been watching me watch her cleavage. I experienced a quick in-take of breath, my hormonal apnea, and then I looked away. I pined for Sara. She haunted the rest of my school day, she haunted my after-school activities, but most of all, she haunted my nights.

A few weeks later, my cousin called to tell me that Sara liked me and wanted me to ask her to homecoming. My cousin never called, and so my mother, who waited downstairs for me, was suspicious. I knew that when the conversation was over, I would have to answer a litany of questions: What did she want? Why was she calling? My mother liked my cousin, but my mother was also attuned to the nuances of my daily life—who I talked to, who I didn't. Even as I spoke to my cousin, I was trying to come up with answers that would satisfy my mother. What my cousin wanted to know—her reason for calling—was if I liked Sara.

"Well? Do you?"

"Sure," I said. "She's okay. What do you mean by *like*?"

"You know," she said. "Do you *like* her? Do you think she's *cute*?"

"I guess so," I said. "I mean, there are other cute girls, too. She's okay. Sure."

"Just okay? She says you're always looking at her."

"That's crazy," I said. "Looking at her?" I laughed.

"Well," my cousin said, "what do you think? Do you want to ask her to homecoming?"

"I don't know," I said. "Maybe. Let me think about it."

I wanted to ask Sara to homecoming. Oh, God, I wanted to. But I didn't. In fact, I made sure not to look at her again, either. I had to push all of her—her wild hair, her cleavage—far from my mind.

In addition to my crippling shyness, I was also fearful of rejection, fearful of the accompanying humiliation. Even though it had been confirmed that this girl liked me, this information had been received secondhand, so there was a fraction of a percent chance that she might tell me to go to hell. And that was enough for me to justify shutting her out. For the remainder of sophomore year, she radiated annoyance each day when I walked into our dramatic arts class. I didn't even have to look at her; I could feel it. I spent homecoming day at the Ford City Mall movie theater. I paid for the first movie, then sneaked into the next two. I went alone, because that's what lonely guys do: They go to movies alone while everyone else is out having fun.

The good news was, my hair had never looked better. For those first two years of high school, my coif put up no arguments. By and large, I was able to tame it using a hair dryer and without having to resort to various sprays. I kept it not too long and not too short. Mostly, I wore it parted in the middle. These were the good years for me and my hair, the salad days. But then something happened. Between my sophomore and junior year, a latent gene must have awakened. This occurred after a haircut. For some reason, I was unable to part my hair in the middle anymore. It just didn't work. The beautician suggested combing it straight back. It was a new look—and, in all honesty, it didn't look bad (really, it didn't)—so I casually agreed to it. Little did I realize that I would never be able to part my hair down the middle again—ever! My parting days were over. My hair, which had struggled for control throughout all of grammar school, had laid low for the first two years of high school only to return with a master plan that would finally put an end to this business of trying to be cool.

But while my hair was still looking reasonably good—combed back but stylish—I began to woo a girl named Beckie, and by the spring of my junior year, we were a couple. She and I had found in each other those physical idiosyncrasies that we liked to wonder over. For me, it was her nose. It was a puggish nose with no discernable cartilage, and so I liked to press it down with my thumb until it was almost flat against her face.

"That doesn't hurt?" I'd ask.

"Nope," she'd say. For her, it was my hair. "My stud," she would say, running her fingers through it. "Look at your studly hairdo." We were, I had thought, a couple for the ages.

One day, while I was sitting at my kitchen table, Beckie walked behind me to mess with my hair. My mother was cooking dinner. The fluorescent lights were bright, unforgiving. Beckie touched my hair. She thumbed the crown of my head.

"How cute," she said.

"What?"

"There's a tiny bald spot here," she said.

"What? No there's not."

"Mrs. McNally," she said. "Come here. Look."

My mother walked over, next to Beckie, and parted the hair on my crown. (For the record, my mother was the least sentimental person I have ever known.) "She's right," my mother said. "You've got a bald spot."

I had spent my entire life pushing aside any and all empirical evidence that confronted me. My father was bald; my brother was going bald; a few uncles on my mother's side were bald. I was convinced, however, that I would not go bald. I'd always had hair—lots of it!—and so the idea of not having hair seemed preposterous. I'm sure this is how rich people think before losing all their money in a bad investment. I'll never be poor! they think, and then, a few years later, they jump off the roof of the tallest building in town.

"Quit touching it," I said, dodging everyone's fingers. "You'll only make it worse."

After the bald spot, which was probably no bigger than a dime, had been revealed, there was no going back: It would only get larger. Beckie and I began to argue. We never mentioned the bald spot again, but it had come between us. If Beckie wanted to go one place, I wanted to go another. If I liked a new song, she didn't.

The end came a few weeks later, in the front seat of my mother's Ford LTD, in the parking lot of R&D's, a grim little ice cream shop where we often went for milkshakes. I had already bought us the shakes when she finally broached the subject. "There's something we need to talk about," she began. Even as she gave her reasons for ending it, she absently picked lint off my shirt and straightened it with her palm. I realize now how to interpret these gestures, that I was being cleaned up before being sent out into the world. Many years later, when my first wife began picking lint from my shirt and straightening it with her palm, I knew we didn't have much longer together.

I spent my post-Beckie days in a funk. It was the August before the start of my senior year. A new movie had just come out: *Fast Times at Ridgemont High*. No movie spoke to me more than this one. I would stay in the theater after it had ended and then watch it a second, sometimes a third time. I returned to it, day after day, until I ran out of money. One afternoon, I was short a dime and stood outside the movie theater, asking if anyone could spare some change. I was sixteen years old, going bald, and begging for money. Who knew my fall would come this fast, this hard?

On the day of my senior picture, I couldn't get my hair to do what I wanted it to do. It was too poofy, too odd looking. I wanted to stay home from school, but my mother wouldn't have it. "Not for your hair," she said. I showed up late, miserable. In my photo, I'm trying to smile, but you could see it in my eyes: I'm depressed. My hair, on the other hand, is clearly enjoying this victorious moment. It is a crazy red pompadour, about four inches too high and absurdly wavy, not at all a look I would consciously have given myself. Who, except for a bottom-rung Elvis impersonator, would have?

As I write this I am, by any objective and honest account, bald. I eventually had to admit defeat, as do all bald guys, except for those who try comb-overs or pay for plugs. I refuse to go that route. I've worn baseball caps for years—first to hide the baldness, then out of mere habit. On those days when I don't wear one, I'll reach up to adjust it, only to realize that something's missing from my head.

As with the tiny bald spot, it's difficult to see the whole story when you stand too close. Isolated memories are like the dots of an impressionistic painting. This dot is orange; that dot is green. This dot is about love; that dot is about fear. Only when you stand back and see how the clusters of dots look together do you see the larger painting. This memoir began as dots, but the more dots I explored, the more I began to see the broader landscape—the portrait of a boy whose appetites, both literal and figurative, are large and whose heart is always yearning for more than he has. And so the arrangement of this book is the arrangement of memory itself: seemingly free-floating but connected by the same undercurrent of desires, wants, weaknesses. If my school photos were a deck of cards, this memoir is me shuffling them, flipping one over, studying it, and then shuffling them again, flipping over another photo, and so on, until the larger story forms.

Every story must begin somewhere, so imagine a boy. Imagine he's you. Only once during the entirety of your grade school career do you arrive in the morning before anyone else has shown up. You have the entire blacktop to yourself. It's magical, really. The idea of being the first to show up has never occurred to you. Who normally shows up first? You have no idea. The season is fall, but it's inching into winter. The sky is dark; the moon is still visible. And then, as the sun begins to rise, your classmates appear, the ones who make your heart race with yearning, the ones who make your heart race from fear, the ones you don't even notice though you must surely see them every day, the ones you notice every morning if only because they are the lonely standouts. Soon they are all here. The sky is getting ever-so-slightly brighter, but the moon remains. It's one of the strangest things you've ever seen, the moon and the sun both visible, and you want to point it out to everyone, but you keep it to yourself. Like so many other moments from your life, you'll save it. Quietly. Tuck it away. Collect it. This moment; this dot. Little do you realize you'll remember this morning for the rest of your life. Little do you realize that each day is a small miracle full of every imaginable horror and beauty. You pull down your knit cap and go stand in your designated line, and then you wait your turn as the great march indoors begins, the school day officially commencing.

PART ONE
The Fat Boy's Home

COURTING DISASTER

Barbara was the first woman I had a crush on. She was in her thirties, divorced, drove a '66 Mustang, and lived in the mobile home across the street. She and my mother would stand outside, near our trailer's propane tanks, and smoke Winstons. Summers, she wore shorts and cheap flip-flops and loose cotton blouses unbuttoned low. "You like my car?" she asked me one hot, dusty day. "As soon as you can drive, I'll give it to you."

I was three years old. My own vehicle was a Batmobile pedal car that I rode feverishly around the trailer court. I liked riding my Batmobile right up to Barbara's painted toenails. From my seated perspective, I would get dizzy looking up at Barbara, waiting for her to bend down and touch the top of my head. Even the sight of her Mustang parked next to her trailer made my heart pound harder because I knew that this meant she was home.

We lived in Guidish Park Mobile Homes, in a southwest suburb of Chicago, from 1966 until 1969. I was born in late 1965, so I remember nothing about my life before the trailer court. The trailer court is where my memory begins: my daily life finally, at long last, coming into focus. But my memories now of those years are like a reel of miscellaneous film footage spliced together—a few frames here, an actual full-blown scene there, very little of it cohesive.

One of my earliest memories (one of the few extended ones) is of me sitting in my Batmobile while my mother and Barbara talked. My mother looked down and said, "Johnny. Go inside and get me my cigarettes."

I didn't want to leave Barbara, but I also didn't want to disobey my mother, so I climbed out of the Batmobile and ran to the trailer, mounting the concrete block steps leading to the only entrance. My mother always kept her cigarettes in a special case that snapped on top and held a lighter in a pouch like a kangaroo carrying its baby. For years, my go-to Mother's Day present would be a new cigarette case.

Cigarettes in hand, I hurried back outside and gave them to my mother. And then I started chattering on about my Hot Wheels, telling Barbara that I had a Hot Wheel that looked just like her car, and I wondered if maybe she'd like to see it. It was a purple custom Mustang, and it was my favorite.

"Johnny," my mother said. "The adults are talking."

Barbara said, "Another time, sweetie," and winked at me. I loved this woman. I truly did.

•

As early as I can remember, I had wanted to be a special little boy, a boy who did spectacular things, but for the life of me I couldn't think of any spectacular things to do, so I played with my Hot Wheels instead and let my imaginary characters who drove those little cars do all the brave and amazing things that I wished I could be doing—fighting bad guys, surviving cataclysmic events, and saving lives.

•

In the trailer next door lived a man I called Grandpa. Both of my real grandfathers and one grandmother had died before I was born, so the old guy living next door was the next best thing. He was a retired lineman for the electric company and was missing several fingers, which fascinated me. He'd let me look at the stumps and study them. We also had secrets, Grandpa and I. He would take me into his bedroom and show me a billy club hanging on a bedpost from a leather strap.

"This is my nigger beater," he said. "Some nigger comes in here to rob me, I'll take care of the son of a bitch. Believe you me."

He made me promise not to tell my mother what he had said or that he had shown me his weapon. I nodded. Of course I wouldn't. For one thing, I had no idea what he was talking about. I was three years old. He was speaking gibberish, using words I'd never heard. He showed me his collection of knives, too. He talked about his son being a worthless bastard. He told me I was a good kid because I didn't talk much.

"I don't like kids unless they're quiet," he said.

My mother wasn't fond of Grandpa. She hated how he would call me over to share his TV dinner and then complain about it later, accusing me of eating all of his food.

"I want to strangle that man," she would say, but she felt sorry for him because his own son wouldn't talk to him or bring his grandkids to visit him. She believed that he really did care for me, that I was the closest thing to family that he had. "Still," she would say, "I wouldn't mind choking him."

It was Grandpa who taught me how to court a girl.

"See her," he said as the two of us peeked out from a window inside his trailer. He nodded toward a girl named Patty. Patty was a chunky girl, probably three years older than me. Grandpa said, "You want to get a girl's attention?"

I nodded, thinking of lovely Barbara and her Mustang.

Grandpa handed me a pair of scissors and said, "Call her 'Fatty Patty' and then chase her with the scissors." Then he added, "But don't tell your mother."

"Okay," I said.

This sounded like great fun. Normally I played by myself, but the thought of chasing someone with scissors thrilled me.

Grandpa slowly opened his front door for me to exit. Once outside, I held the scissors up over my head and yelled, "Fatty Patty!"

Startled, Patty looked up, saw me (a wide-eyed neighbor boy holding scissors over his head), and screamed.

"Fatty Patty!" I yelled louder and charged down the concrete block steps toward her. Patty screamed again and ran away.

I chased her between trailers, across gravel driveways, and onto another street populated with people I didn't know. And then I lost sight of her. I was panting, the scissors still over my head. I heard Grandpa calling my name, so I returned, heart thumping, grinning.

"You did good," Grandpa said. "She'll never forget you."

"Fatty Patty," I said and laughed.

Grandpa laughed and said, "You hungry? Want to split a TV dinner with me?"

"Sure," I said.

Together, we ate Salisbury steak and mashed potatoes. He gave me sips of his coffee.

"You should have seen the look on her face," Grandpa said. He laughed louder. I'd never seen him so happy. "Serves her right," he said.

"Serves her right," I repeated.

•

Oh, how I wanted to give Barbara a ride in my Batmobile. Oh, how I wanted her to give me a ride in her Mustang. I wanted to hold her, sit in her lap, sleep against her. Forty years later, when I asked my father if there was, in fact, a woman named Barbara who lived near us and drove a Mustang, he said, "Barbara?" His eyes widened. "Oh, hell, yeah. She was a good-looking woman, too." He paused, as though stunned by his own memory of her, a memory that I had resurrected by providing only the barest of facts. Staring beyond me, he shook his head and said, "Damn fine-looking woman."

•

"I hated that trailer," my mother told me years later. "I used to wish it would burn down. Every day I wished that."

•

My Batmobile was my prized possession. Given my parents' income, the Batmobile must have been an extravagant gift. I stowed the fake automobile each night in an aluminum shed that sat in the driveway. In the driveway also sat a white 1966 Rambler, a stick shift with no air conditioner, and a VW van with no air conditioner or heater. A vehicle without a heater in Chicago was a monumental disaster, and to this day I have no idea what my father could possibly have been thinking when he bought it.

One Saturday morning, I walked out to the shed, opened it, and looked at the empty space where my Batmobile should have been. I stared at the space, trying to make logical sense out of a sight that was illogical. And then I screamed. My father rushed outside, probably expecting to see an abduction in progress.

When I told him what was wrong, my father said, "Son of a bitch." He looked around as though the culprits were in sight, then said, "Come with me."

Dad and I walked up and down each row of the trailer court. Four rows away, I saw three boys standing over the Batmobile. "Look," I whispered. But even at three years old I knew it was possible for more than one boy in the trailer court to own a Batmobile.

There weren't many actual lawns where we lived, and the few lawns that did exist were mere postage stamp lots. This particular lawn had a fence surrounding it, but it couldn't have been very high.

My father yelled to the boys, "Hey! Where the hell did you get that?"

"It's mine," one of the boys said.

"The hell it is," my father said. Like a giant, my father stepped over the fence, walked over to the boys, and picked up the Batmobile with one hand. The entire time I thought, *But he said it was his*, and my fear was that we were now thieves. My father stepped back over the fence and set the Batmobile down.

"Go on," he said to me. "Ride it home."

I was too afraid to look back at the boys we may have just robbed. I sat down in the Batmobile and started pedaling, keeping pace with my father, who said nothing as we made our way back to the trailer.

•

My days back then had a distinct rhythm. While my father was away cleaning strangers' rugs or washing their walls, I stayed with my mother and played with my Hot Wheels. At some point in the early afternoon, my mother and Barbara would have a smoke by the propane tanks, and I would stare longingly up at Barbara, who would look down at me and smile while my mother was talking. Grandpa would eventually call me over to share a meal with him and then complain about it to my mother. When my father came home, my mother would head to work at a factory that made corrugated boxes. With my mother gone, my father might listen to Herb Alpert's "Tijuana Taxi" on the record player or the theme to *Peter Gunn*. My brother, who was six years older, had his own life, and I don't remember seeing him around much in those days. At night, my mother and I slept at one end of the trailer while my father and my brother slept at the other end. I don't know why my parents had made this arrangement. Perhaps because I couldn't sleep in a room without my mother, to whom I was irrationally attached when I was three. Or maybe there were problems in the marriage. Just as I was unaware of Grandpa's racism, I was also unaware of my mother's deep unhappiness. I was unaware of most things, it turned out.

•

If you read about trailer fires, you'll likely see the word *firetrap*; and of the occupants' fates, you will often read, "They didn't have a chance."

A person has only two to three minutes to extinguish a house fire before it's out of control. A mobile home can burn entirely to the ground in five to ten minutes.

It wouldn't be until 1976 that the construction of mobile homes would be regulated by the government. According to the 2013 report on manufactured home fires by the National Fire Protection Association, "The death rate was 57% lower for post-standard manufactured homes than for pre-standard manufactured homes."

A fire in Batavia, New York, that took place in November of 1969 brings home the perils of preregulation mobile homes. According to a newspaper article, a neighbor heard screams for help coming from a nearby trailer at four in the morning. When she ran outside, the trailer was already overcome with flames. She tried opening the door but couldn't. She awoke another neighbor, who called the fire department, but there was nothing left to do when they got there but put out the flames that had, according to a reporter, "melted much of the aluminum shell of the unit." The cause of the fire was not determined. It could have been an electric heater. It could have been a small gas stove. It could have been an oil-fired furnace. The newspaper reports, "Mr. Beakman, whose shouts had awakened Mrs. Piche, was found dead near the door at the front of the trailer. His wife's body was found in the hallway between the bedrooms at the rear of the trailer and Mrs. Ogden was found in bed in another bedroom near the center of the structure. All had died of smoke inhalation."

•

In late October of 1969, two weeks before I turned four, my mother got her wish. Our trailer burned down.

Here's what I remember: Coughing and coughing, unable to get comfortable. It was night. My coughing, deep and croupy, woke my mother, and my mother, unable to see through the smoke, screamed for my father. My mother carried me to the other end of the trailer and then, gathering my brother, took us outside while my father, to my mother's irritation, mystifyingly changed out of his pajamas and into a pair of jeans and a shirt. My mother hurried us to Grandpa's trailer, pounding on his door and waking him up. Perhaps thinking they had finally come for him—*they* being all the black people who were going to descend on the trailer court to rob him—Grandpa answered the door holding his billy club.

While my mother used Grandpa's phone to call the fire department, my brother and I stood side by side and stared through a window at our trailer. At first, all I saw was smoke pouring from the seams and the occasional flickering of flames inside.

In the few seconds before the fire overwhelmed the trailer, my father threw three things outside: a birdcage inside of which lived a finch named Dale, a Code-a-Phone answering machine, and a Von Schrader rug cleaner. And then, flames at his back, he leaped from the trailer, landing on his knees.

This is where my memory switches from grainy fragments to full-blown Technicolor. It's a clear dividing line in my life: before the trailer fire and after the trailer fire. It's like switching from a tiny black-and-white TV with rabbit ears to a high-definition color TV the size of a wall. The first four years of my life was like a short picaresque novel populated with odd neighbors and the occasional recurring relative. The fire, however, was like landing in Oz. It's when my subconscious and conscious minds finally clicked into place, one layered over the other, like the sun and moon during a lunar eclipse. As I watched the fire, I was keenly aware of what was happening around me. I felt, for the first time in my short life, like a sentient being and, thus, truly alive.

•

My father joined us at Grandpa's after saving the bird, the answering machine, and the rug cleaner. From Grandpa's window, I watched our trailer door fall off its hinges as though in slow motion. The flames lit up the trailer court. Once sparks began spitting on Grandpa's window, making a loud popping sound each time one struck glass, my mother took us across the street to Barbara's trailer.

The firemen, I learned many years later, were volunteer, and one of the reasons it took so long for the trucks to arrive was because the trailer was in an unincorporated area and there was confusion as to whose responsibility we were. The trailer was destroyed by the time they arrived and likely would have been destroyed no matter which fire station responded, although the fire itself continued to burn. There came a point while trying to extinguish the flames when the firemen had to stop working because of a series of explosions coming from within the trailer.

"What do you have in there?" one of them asked my father. "Fireworks? Ammunition?"

"Why the hell would I have fireworks in there?" my father asked. Then: "Oh, wait. I know what it is."

My parents had stored jugs of wine under the kitchen sink, and, one by one, the bottles exploded from the heat.

My mother and father argued at sunrise when Red Cross arrived to help us. The Red Cross representatives had come with clothes and $165 in cash. My father refused their help. His own father had served in World War II and had claimed that Red Cross charged servicemen for coffee. This was, in my father's eyes, reason enough to turn them down. My mother, the more pragmatic of the two and often exasperated at my father, signed whatever papers Red Cross had asked her to sign. She welcomed their help.

By morning, all that remained of our home was a smoking heap of twisted metal and ashes, but before the sun came up and while the fire trucks remained outside, their lights swirling and swirling, I fell asleep in Barbara's lap while she sang to me. Although we had lost pretty much everything we owned, I was a happy little boy.

•

572 degrees Fahrenheit is the temperature at which human tissue begins to combust.

801 degrees Fahrenheit is the average temperature on Mercury, the planet closest to the Sun.

1,100 degrees Fahrenheit is the average temperature at which a house fire burns.

1,400 to 1,800 degrees Fahrenheit is the temperature required to cremate a body, after which only bone fragments remain.

•

Several days after the fire, I walked through the ruins and studied everything that had melted. I had the taste of rotten eggs at the back of my throat, likely from smoke inhalation, and I felt queasy each time I swallowed.

At the spot where I kept my Hot Wheels in a tiny plastic garbage can was a mound of melted metal. I could make out a few of the cars' shapes, but they were now merely part of some larger, misshapen object. It was the sight of my little cars, which I played with every day, that brought home the import of what had happened to us. Until then, it had all been a grand, surreal adventure.

Near the end of our trip, my father found the only possession that survived the fire intact: a wooden nineteenth-century crucifix that had once belonged to his mother. It lay in a bedroom closet, underneath a pile of ash. The crucifix, however, was unscathed except for the edges of the cross, which had blackened. My mother always interpreted the crucifix's survival as evidence of a higher being. I tend to think that the crucifix had been soaked in some kind of flame retardant, although I honestly have no idea how it survived while everything else perished. For years, whenever I wanted to return to the night of the fire, I would hold the crucifix up to my nose and breathe in the smell of smoke that it still retained, and the aftermath of that night would instantly come back.

•

"Every day," my mother said when I was nine, "I wished that trailer would burn down."

She confessed this right after she told me that Grandpa had died. I felt nothing at this news. I had seen him only one more time when he came to visit us at my aunt's house a month after the fire. Mostly he complained that the fire had damaged his window and that my parents still owed him money for it. I have a Polaroid from his visit: I'm sitting on his lap and the two of us are smiling, my mouth rimmed purple from the grape punch I had been drinking. As for Barbara, I never saw her again, and she never gave me her Mustang. I couldn't say what became of her, but I eventually fell in love with other women, dozens of them, including my kindergarten teacher, Miss Mendoza, along with many of my classmates, until the pool of women I loved shrunk and shrunk as I got older and older.

I still remember trying to sleep as the trailer filled with smoke that night. I kept coughing, unable to catch my breath, and there was a horrible noise coming from my throat. I coughed and coughed until my mother shook me awake, and then I opened my eyes into thick smoke. My eyes burned, but I could see in the distance, through the smoke, flickering light from a half-open door in the hallway. It was like waking into a dream. Or death. My mother picked me up as though I weighed nothing. Within seconds, we were out of the trailer, along with my brother.

Had I not coughed, it was unlikely anyone would have woken up that night. Or so I told myself.

On the day that my mother confessed to me that she had wished the trailer would burn down, we were driving to a grocery store. It was summer, the car's windows were rolled up, and my mother was smoking. I stared at my mother. Had my mother set fire to the trailer? I knew she hadn't, but I couldn't not entertain the possibility.

The grocery store, Dominick's, was across the street from our old trailer court. I looked toward it every single time we drove by, wondering if anyone would remember the boy who had pedaled his Batmobile up and down the street or chased a little girl with scissors but who also, on what could have been his very last night of sleep, saved his family, becoming, for the only time in his life, the hero of his own story. My mother, on the other hand, never looked, even on the day she confessed her secret to me. It was as though the trailer court had ceased to exist, as though we had not all almost died that late October night of 1969. But I knew better. I knew the opposite was true.

My mother crushed her cigarette in the ashtray. Country music was on the radio. A Charley Pride song might have been playing. Or something by Tammy Wynette, a twangy song about heartbreak and independence. Unlike my father, who talked and talked and talked, my mother was often silent. If I'd asked her what she had been think-ing, she'd have shook her head and said, "Nothing," even as visions of flames filled her mind, the four of us trapped inside a burning trailer. My mother believed in karmic retribution.

"Be careful what you wish for," she told tell me as she pulled into the grocery store parking lot. In her version of the story, I wasn't a hero. She was the villain. "Be very careful," she added, as though my future truly depended upon such silent longings, those darkest of desires we keep to ourselves.

THE GENIUS AND I

Jimmy Finger lived in the apartment directly above. It was 1973, and I was seven. Jimmy was two years older and attended what his mother called the "special school," suggesting that Jimmy went there because he was a genius. And he looked like a genius to me: plastic-framed glasses, uncombed hair, filthy clothes. In the only photo that I have of him, he looks like he's trapped inside of an invisible jail cell. He's screaming, his arms are raised over his head as though he's pounding at bars no one can see, and his glasses are crooked. He looks like an insane genius. Or maybe he just looks insane.

That summer I spent my days listening to Chicago radio stations on a transistor radio and messing around with my portable cassette player, which was about the size of a shoebox. Sometimes I would plug in the cassette player's microphone, hold it close to my transistor radio's speaker, and record songs onto a blank cassette—top forty hits like "Bad, Bad Leroy Brown" and "The Morning After." When I played the tape back later, I could sometimes hear my mother talking in the background or a neighbor's dog barking.

That was also the summer when I realized that I could use my cassette player to record my own improvisational comedy shows, so I invited Jimmy Finger down, and together we did our best impersonations of *The Honeymooner*'s characters Ralph Kramden and Ed Norton. I was Norton, probably because I liked saying, in that goofy Art Carney voice, "Hey, Ralphie boy!" Or maybe I was Norton because Jimmy Finger liked screaming, "Bang! Zoom! To the moon!" I had a package of three blank sixty-minute cassette tapes, the cheap kind from Kmart with orange labels, and we filled up all three hours in one sitting.

Our Ralph and Norton personas carried over into our regular friendship so that I might be at the kitchen table eating a bowl of cereal when I would hear Jimmy scream, "Norton!" I would run to a window, open it wide, poke my head out, look up, and there he would be: Jimmy Finger in character, peering down at me. He would say something else in his exasperated Jackie Gleason voice, like, "Get. Down. Stairs. *Now!*" and I would reply, "Right away, Ralphie boy!"

We always met on the sidewalk behind the apartment, sometimes as Ralph and Norton but more often as ourselves, and then we rode our bikes around the neighborhood in search of Dumpsters. I wasn't afraid of bugs back then or green flies or disease or other people's garbage bags or crud. Starting with the Dumpster that belonged to our apartment building, we'd lift lids with the hope that riches awaited us. Sometimes, we'd find an old radio. Other times, a stack of albums. It was stunning, really, how much worthwhile stuff people threw out.

Jimmy Finger collected old doorknobs. He liked to tinker with them, taking them apart and putting them back together again, figuring out how they worked. He also collected anything that had a cord. It didn't matter if it worked or not, if the plastic shell of the appliance was broken, if it looked as though it had caught fire. If it had a cord, he wanted it. He stowed all of his electrical items in his family's storage unit in the laundry room, and that's where he spent most of his time— in the basement. There were long stretches when the storage locker was the first place I'd go to look for Jimmy.

My mother, convinced that he was actually living down there, said, "He's going to burn this place down."

I shrugged. Probably, I thought. But since I would have been partly responsible as his conspirator, helping him carry the electronics home and down into the basement, I said nothing one way or the other. Better to let him burn down the apartment, I figured, than to admit my guilt.

•

By the time I was thirteen, my family had moved us to nine different places, mostly apartment buildings. My friends during those years tended to be friends not because we were the same age or had common interests but rather because we lived near each other. This was especially true in apartment buildings, where many of the tenants were childless. You ended up friends with another boy or girl because they were the only other boy or girl remotely near your age. And if you weren't friends, you were enemies. There was little in-between.

Jimmy liked me, I'm sure, because I was younger and didn't pick on him. Furthermore, I believed his mother's story that he was a genius, I enjoyed looking in Dumpsters, and I never tried to take over the role of Ralph Kramden. In fact, I *liked* being Norton. It was, in this regard, a mutually beneficial friendship.

But Jimmy had friends I didn't care for, like Dale, who also attended the special school but who was older than both of us and taller by about a foot. And Dale didn't look like a genius. He looked like a child version of a patient in *One Flew over the Cuckoo's Nest*. One day, while Jimmy and I were using long sticks to move bags of garbage around inside a Dumpster as though the bags were bloated corpses, Dale showed up with a can of orange spray paint. The whole time he stood there, he shook the can. I could hear the ball inside clicking with each shake. When I asked Dale what he was going to do with the spray paint, he raised the can and sprayed my face with it.

I dropped my stick and ran back to my apartment. My mother cleaned my face, but my father raged on about how he was going to kill the kid who'd done this to me.

"Who is he?" he asked.

"Dale."

"Who's Dale?"

"Friend of Jimmy's."

"Why the hell are you hanging out with someone like him?" my father asked.

"I wasn't hanging around with him!" I yelled.

"Hey!" my father said, his voice sharp. "Don't take that tone with me!"

"Bob," my mother said, trying to let him know that he was heading down the wrong path and should ease back, but my father wouldn't have any of it.

"Don't *Bob* me, goddamn it," he said. To me, he said, "Come on. I want you to point him out to me."

I didn't want to—I feared Dale doing something worse the next time, like spraying me with the paint while flicking a lighter, turning the spray can into a flame torch—but I always felt helpless when my father got it in his head that there was retribution to be paid and that he was going to dole out the punishment.

In the end, my father was unable to get any satisfaction. Dale denied it, and Dale's father claimed that I was the boy who was stirring up trouble. My father took me to the police station to file a complaint, but no one at the police station was all that interested, either.

"Son of a bitch," my father said when we got back into his truck. "You let me know next time that asshole comes around, you hear me?" But I never did, and my father eventually let it go.

•

One afternoon, Jimmy showed up at my door looking more disheveled than usual. I started talking to him in my Art Carney voice, but Jimmy didn't offer up Jackie Gleason in return. He motioned with his head for me to follow him, so I did—down the stairs, out the back door, and onto the shady sidewalk. He looked up—the windows to both of our apartments were above us—so he motioned with his head again, and I followed him to the Dumpster, out of our parents' earshot.

"I found an abandoned house," he said. "They left everything inside it, too."

"What?"

I stared at Jimmy. I heard what he was saying, but the words weren't making logical sense.

"We can take whatever we want," Jimmy said.

"Really?" I asked.

"Yeah. But we gotta hurry."

The house was located outside my legal perimeter, but I decided the risk was worth taking. I followed Jimmy, who rode a three-speed bike with a sissy bar. Attached to the sissy bar by a rope was a Radio Flyer wagon. My bike, a hand me down, was as old as me and had been stolen once, but then I found it a year later chained to a fence. It had been spray-painted black, and the original handlebars had been replaced by the kind that curled at either end. It looked like a bicycle you'd see someone riding around in a third world country, or a vehicle that had barely survived the apocalypse. Naturally, I loved it.

The genius and I parked our bikes in the backyard and entered through the rear door. Jimmy was right: Everything was in place, as though the family had simply run away in the middle of the night. My parents sometimes moved from our apartments in the middle of the night, but we always took everything with us. Not so here. This house was everything Jimmy had promised. Even the clock on the wall still ticked, as though to say, "Hell. Lo. Hell. Lo. Hell. Lo. Take. This. Take. That. It's. Yours. It's. Yours. All. Yours."

"Help me carry the TV," Jimmy said, and I obeyed.

Next, Jimmy needed a hand with a heavy antique radio. My job, I was coming to realize, was to take orders from Jimmy Finger about which items to place in his wagon, and I played along, hoping that he would share his riches with me.

"Careful," Jimmy said. "Don't drop it."

"Okie doke, Ralphie boy!" I said, doing a limp-legged Art Carney impression, but Jimmy Finger cut me short with a look. It was a look unlike any he'd given me before. This is serious, the look said.

We made several trips from the house to our apartment, loading the goods inside Jimmy's parents' storage locker. A blender. Lamps. CorningWare. You name it. We worked through dinner, until it was dark out. Crickets stopped chirping each time we'd walk outside to load more onto the wagon. I had a feeling that other people, hearing news of an abandoned house, would descend on us at any moment, but no one did. I was happy for that. What we were doing was addictive. The more things we took away, the more things I *wanted* to take away.

On our final trip of the night, as we headed home in the dark with the last load of abandoned treasures, a familiar car pulled up beside me. I was sweaty and overheated. Exhausted. I think I know that car, I thought. The window rolled down. The man driving the car was my father, and the car was ours. The green dashboard lights lit up his face, giving him a particularly sinister look. He glanced at Jimmy and then at Jimmy's wagon, which was overflowing with things a boy Jimmy's age would not have had any use for, but then my father directed his green-hued attention at me again.

"Get your ass home. Now!" he ordered.

Back in our apartment, I was told that I was grounded for an indeterminate period of time and that I would only be able to leave my bedroom for meals. My father didn't know where I had been that night or what I had been doing, and for years neither did I. I had believed what I wanted to believe—that the house was abandoned and that I had done nothing wrong. But one night twenty years later I woke up in a sweat, wondering what the family thought when they returned from vacation to find that their house had been raided by two criminal masterminds they could never have imagined, one of whom, at fifty years old, would still be living with his parents, the other of whom would become a professor and a writer but who, on the night of the robbery, clutched a stuffed bear and cried himself to sleep, worried that he would be condemned to his bedroom forever, never to see the light of day again.

WORKING STIFF

I started working when I was six.

My father had taken me to a flea market to help sell some of his crap, and I gathered together some of my own crap to sell, including a large yellow toy dump truck. The flea market took place on the dusty gravel parking lot of a drive-in movie theater. While my father was busy talking to a customer at the other end of the table, a mother with a small child stepped up to examine our goods. The child, who was at least three years younger than me, started playing with the truck, so I cleared my throat, ready to yell out the toy's price in case either one asked me. Before I could say anything, however, they walked away. To my horror, the child took my dump truck with him.

At first I assumed that the mother didn't know what her horrible thieving spawn had done, but when she looked down at him and then back at me, who was glaring but not saying anything, I understood that the mother was complicit. They were a team, like Bonnie and Clyde, but instead of being lovers, as they were in the movie I had seen at the very drive-in I now stood in, they were mother and son.

Not only did I not make any money that day, but I was in the hole, where I would remain pretty much the rest of my life.

•

Despite this setback, I continued selling junk with my father at the flea market. I also supplemented my income whenever an opportunity arose, like those times my father offered a quarter for each pimple I popped on his back. This proved to be a short-term occupation since my father's back was vexed with hideous pimples for only a short period, but as a seven-year-old, I saw nothing disgusting or unusual about my task. On a good day, I might walk away with a five dollar bill. All profit.

But my primary income remained selling crap. After a few brutal Chicago winters that involved selling at indoor flea markets where we'd lug boxes across treacherous, icy parking lots in subzero weather, I negotiated a flat fee with my father rather than continuing to sell off my own toys. In exchange for my services, I would receive five dollars per workday—a respectable salary in 1975 for a nine-year-old.

That same year, we had moved from an apartment into a condominium, and in order to feed my record-buying appetite, I went door to door and offered my dog-walking services to my new neighbors for the very reasonable fee of five dollars a week. I secured two clients, which brought my weekly salary up to twenty dollars, my monthly up to eighty.

Weekdays, I walked Ralph and Moo. Weekends, I sold crap at flea markets. I had come to realize that my father paid me not so much for my help but so that I could be a captive audience for his monologues that would go on for hours and hours. He talked about what kinds of things he might buy wholesale to sell, and one time he laid out his plans for how he was going to renovate a bread delivery truck into a walk-in store, complete with shelves full of merchandise.

These soliloquies drove me to consider opening the door of the van and jumping out while it was moving at sixty miles an hour. I couldn't bear listening to them. The van didn't have a passenger seat, so I sat on the floor, unbuckled, and leaned against a sheet of plywood that separated the front of the van from the back. I would sit there and wonder if the locked door would come unlocked if I pulled the handle. If so, I would roll out onto the side the road. For the duration of the drive, which was often two hours or longer, I would weigh the benefits and disadvantages of going through with my plan. The whole while, my father would continue talking, every so often saying, "Huh? You say something?"

"No, Dad. I didn't say anything."

"Huh? What was that?"

"I didn't say anything!"

"Okay, goddamn it. Watch your tone. I'm your father, in case you forgot."

Once, I brought along a copy of *Mad Magazine* to read on the drive, but I had no sooner opened it up when my father said, "Fine. I guess I'm boring you. Don't listen to me then."

I lied. I said, "You're not boring me, Dad."

"Then why the hell aren't you listening?"

I looked at the door handle. More than ever before, I wanted to pull that handle, open the door, and jump out. I wanted to roll into a ditch and start running. But I was too much of a coward to go through with it, which is a good thing, since I would likely have died upon impact.

Another time, I brought a cassette player to the flea market so I could at least listen to music while we sat in the drive-in's dusty parking lot. I needed it to drown out my father's voice. But shortly after I pressed the play button, my father said, "Turn that down, for Christ's sake."

I turned it down. During a drum-heavy moment in the song, I started playing the air drums.

My father glanced over at me with an expression I had never seen before. The next time he glanced over, he said, "Stop doing that. It's embarrassing."

I was ten. My eyes grew warm, but I didn't cry. Embarrassing, I thought. I was embarrassing.

I turned off the music and refused to look at my father the rest of the day. This was the best punishment I could dole out, but it was lost on my father, who launched back into one of his brain-numbing soliloquies as though he hadn't, mere minutes earlier, crushed his son with a look of disgust and a single word.

•

The money I was making wasn't enough.

And so in the seventh grade I started making bootleg cassettes and 8-tracks of newly released albums, which I sold to my classmates.

The reason the tapes lacked a label or any artwork (I explained to anyone interested) was that I had a cousin who worked at Columbia House in Indiana, and they were fresh off the assembly line.

"You want to pay five dollars at a record store?" I asked. "Or do you want to pay me a dollar for the same thing? You decide."

My record collection was such that I could offer a comprehensive selection, but after I delivered the first few tapes, my unhappy customers cried foul and wanted a refund.

"You made these yourself!" one of them said.

"This is your writing on these," someone else said. "You don't have a cousin at Columbia House!"

I tried arguing my case, but it was futile, so I offered refunds to any dissatisfied customers, which turned out to be all of them.

A few weeks later, I began selling knives to my classmates. Not just any kind of knife. These were menacing knives with dragons on their handles and blades six inches long. My father had bought several dozen for us to sell at the flea market, some of which were practical, like the one for scaling fish, and some of which weren't, like the one whose handle had contours to accommodate a clenched fist. Under the guise of building up my own knife collection, I bought several from my father at wholesale prices and then took them to school to sell at a significant markup. I sold a few to boys who were top candidates for murdering me after school, but I didn't care. It was money in my pocket. But before I could sell any more, a teacher saw me flashing a blade on the blacktop before school one morning.

"It's just a knife," I said.

"Hand it over," he said. It was a teacher who knew me but didn't particularly like me because I was a fat kid. He favored the popular kids, not the outcasts or the troublemakers. "Why did you bring this to school?"

"To show a friend," I said.

"Is that all?" he asked. "To show a friend?"

I nodded.

He gave the knife back to me. "Don't bring it back," he said, "or I'll have to take it away."

I nodded again. I put the knife in the front pocket of my Huskies, where it remained for the rest of the school day.

Later that night, I sat in my bedroom, strategizing. I still needed more money, and I still had all these knives I needed to move. I took the knife out of my pocket and practiced flicking it open. The flick was successful only when I heard the lock snap into place. To close the knife, I had to depress the lock with my right thumb while closing the blade with my left hand. I repeated this action, over and over, all the while considering my options—sell the knives after school? Sell them before school?—when the blade got stuck and wouldn't shut.

I pushed the blade harder, but it barely budged. I looked down to see what the problem was, and here's what I saw: half of my forefinger was on one side of the blade while the other half was on the other half of the blade. I had cut my finger in half from the top down.

Two observations:

1) When a knife is extraordinarily sharp, you don't immediately feel pain.

2) A swift, deep cut doesn't bleed right away.

As soon as I removed the knife, my finger began throbbing, and blood pumped out at a startling rate.

At the hospital, I told doctors and nurses that I had cut my finger while slicing open a watermelon. No one believed me, but I stuck to my story so that there was nothing they could do to my parents. I was protecting them. The watermelon story was the best I could come up with. I loved watermelon, after all, and I had recently sliced one open, so there was a ring of truth to it, even though it was unlikely, if not impossible, that I would have cut open my finger doing what I had described.

A doctor stitched my finger back together, and I was released, but the tip of my finger would have no feeling for decades, a constant reminder never to get too enamored with the things that were meant to generate income.

I sold my remaining knives back to my father, who sold them at the flea market, and with my forefinger bandaged in such a way that it looked like a cartoon appendage, I decided to leave the weapons business for good.

•

With the exception of a brief attempt to run his own rug cleaning business, my father was a roofer. He belonged to the roofers' union. He worked with hot tar, mostly. Flat roofs. He started in his teens and took early retirement shortly after my mother died. All told, he was a roofer for over thirty years.

My father rarely made friends with the men from work, but when I was in the sixth grade, my father, mother, and I went to the house of a man named Larry Hunter. In addition to being a roofer, Larry Hunter was an Amway salesman, and the reason we went to his house was to attend an Amway recruitment meeting. My father's idea of the American dream was to make a killing, as he'd have put it, and so he was eager to go to the meeting. Amway, which had long been accused of being a pyramid scheme and was a few years shy of being found guilty of price fixing and making exaggerated income claims, produced a variety of cleaning products for their salesforce to sell at their places of work, to relatives and friends, or door to door, all while recruiting more salespeople.

Larry Hunter's daughters tried to wrangle me into playing a board game with them during the presentation. It would always be a difficult decision for me, deciding which one to follow—girls or money—but that day I followed neither. I followed the weirdness. Weirdness was a powerful pull, and there was no shortage of it that evening in Larry Hunter's living room. Even as a child, standing on the sidelines, I felt the slimy cultishness of Amway as Larry Hunter delivered his speech to a roomful of men and women wearing loud, ill-fitting clothes.

A month later, my father—now a part-time Amway salesman— wasn't seeing the vast profits he'd envisioned while at Larry Hunter's house. This was the promise of failure that I would see repeated throughout my father's life. At the start of each venture—window repair, leather and vinyl repair, gold plating—my father would get a look in his eyes like that of a gambler in an old movie whose face would be superimposed over dollar signs as he drives into Vegas, but only a short while later that look would change to disappointment and then anger, and he would refuse to talk about the failed business.

Six months after the Amway meeting, my father came home from work early, looking unnerved in a way I had never seen before.

His hands were shaking as he lit a Lucky Strike. "That son of a bitch tried to throw me off the roof," he said.

"Who?"

"Hunter," my father said. "He came to work drunk and wanted to fight. And then he tried throwing me off the goddamn roof."

According to my father, some of the other men restrained Larry Hunter so that my father could climb down the ladder. Once on solid ground, my father quit his job and drove to the union hall to put his name in the book. This was what you did when you needed a new job: put your name in the book and waited your turn.

My father stuck to his story that Larry Hunter was drunk, that he was a crazy son of a bitch, but the story never added up for me. Did my father owe him money for Amway products he hadn't sold? Or had my father provoked him? My father wouldn't have hesitated to call him a lying cocksucker to his face, and Larry might have reacted in a way that my father had not expected. I, too, sometimes blurted out insults on the playground, only to realize I'd royally screwed up once the aggrieved party's friends surrounded me later that night on their three-speed Huffys.

Years later, my father and Larry Hunter's path crossed again at a flea market. We were manning our table, and even though years had passed and I had met Larry Hunter only once, I recognized him immediately.

Larry, squinting, approached our table. "Bob? Is that you?"

At the sight of Larry, my father's entire composure changed, like a cornered animal in the wild.

Even as a teenager I was good at reading people, picking up the subtext in a glance or a word, but on that day I saw nothing in Larry Hunter's behavior that suggested that he had once tried to kill my father. In fact, he seemed confused by my father's monosyllabic answers and grunts, by his disinterest to engage.

"Well then," Larry said before walking away. "Good seeing you, Bob. You take care of yourself, you hear?"

My father grunted. Once Larry was out of earshot, my father turned to me and said, "That's the cocksucker who tried pushing me off the roof."

"I know," I said.

I had seen teachers physically abuse students, and I had seen students assault other students, and now I realized that it would be no different once I started a real job.

I would never learn the truth of what happened between my father and Larry Hunter, or if anything had actually happened to prompt Larry Hunter to do what he had done, but I had never seen my father as frightened as he was that day.

"Let's pack up and get the hell out of here," my father said, trying to see which direction Larry Hunter had gone. "Fuck it," he added, tossing our merchandise, even things that were fragile, into boxes without any regard for order.

I didn't argue in favor of staying. I helped my father pack, and in a matter of just a few minutes, we got the hell out of there.

•

The summer between eighth grade and high school, I was offered a three-day gig to be Big Bird for a local car dealership. At six dollars an hour, I would be paid $144 in cash, and no one would be the wiser.

I had already gotten a raise walking dogs, and I still helped my father at the flea market. My total earnings for that month were close to three hundred dollars, the equivalent of almost a thousand dollars today.

The Big Bird job was not without problems. The feathered suit was extraordinarily hot in July. The days were long with few breaks. A high percentage of passengers in passing cars either flipped me off or threw garbage at me. To add insult to injury, the costume didn't really look like Big Bird—I was a bird that was big, but Big Bird I was not. And kids who had come to see Big Bird told me so.

"Your beak doesn't even move," one kid said, and another kid noted with disgust that I sounded nothing like his beloved fictional character.

The benefits outweighed the disadvantages when it came time to take photos with customers. How many cute teenage girls and attractive young mothers sat on my lap? Pretty much everything gave me a boner back then, and if not for the thick, feathered suit, these poor girls and women would have felt Big Bird's weenie pressing against them. Fortunately, they didn't know that inside the costume was a horny, prepubescent boy grunting softly through the screen inside the bird's open beak and that he wanted to dry hump each and every one of them. For this, I was getting paid handsomely. But it was over in three days, and I was back to the slog of my regular routine, waiting for the next big thing to happen.

•

What I had thought would be the next big thing was a book I had spent two years writing and had finally finished the summer between eighth grade and high school. It was a nonfiction book about ol-time comedians—Abbott and Costello, the Three Stooges, Laurel and Hardy, Charlie Chaplin, among others—and I had worked diligently on it, certain that a publisher would snap it up. I had written to publishers, who sent me information about their royalty rates, so I calculated how many books I would need to sell in order to buy my parents a house. I had also written to any living actor or director who'd had any association with the comedians, and several wrote back to me, including Margaret Hamilton, most famous for playing the Wicked Witch of the West but who also appeared in a fairly awful Abbott and Costello movie. I wrote to authors for advice. I wrote to movie studios for information about reprinting photos. I wrote to memorabilia shops in Hollywood to ask for price lists for movie stills. Every day, my parents' mailbox overflowed with letters from long-forgotten movie stars, movie studio legal departments, and fellow writers.

When it came time to submit the book, I closely followed the guidelines for sending query letters to publishers. I sent queries to every publisher in New York as well as a few in Illinois, as a backup. It didn't take long before rejections filled the mailbox, each one saying the same thing, that they didn't accept unsolicited manuscripts. How could this have been? What the hell?

By the end of summer, the book's fate had been sealed, and for a week after that realization, I brooded. But then I started another book. And then another. And then another. And then another.

Twenty-one years after that summer, my first book was finally published, proof that I am nothing if not persistent.

•

The big score did finally come for me and my father. This occurred in 1980 when I suggested that we sell concert T-shirts at the flea market instead of the turquoise and coral jewelry we'd been selling the previous few years. At my suggestion, my father found a guy who found a guy who knew a guy who illegally printed concert T-shirts, and we met the third guy in a parking lot behind McDonald's and bought fifty shirts in a variety of sizes featuring a variety of bands and singers: Bob Seger, Journey, REO Speedwagon, Triumph, etc. The usual.

The first time we took them to a flea market, we sold out.

My father bought several hundred more the next time, and, again, we sold out.

Over the next few years, we sold concert T-shirt and decorative feathers that hung from a strand of leather at the end of which was a roach clip. We quit going to flea markets and traveled instead to city festivals. Corn Festivals. Apple Festivals. Harvest Days Festivals. We went to festivals in Illinois, Michigan, Indiana, and Wisconsin. The entire time, my father never quit talking, even when he'd wake me up at four a.m. so that we could get a prime spot to sell our shirts. And once we were set up, we couldn't keep the shirts in stock. People ate that shit up. But we were also met by religious conservatives in these small, far-flung towns, and they would berate us for promoting the devil's music.

"Hey!" my father would say, leaning across the table, getting in the man or woman's face. "No one's forcing you to buy one. So get the fuck away from our table." Once they were out of earshot, my father would turn to me and say, "Assholes." And then, "Fuck 'em."

●

It was not unusual for me to make a thousand dollars in a weekend. One weekend, we pulled in over three thousand dollars. My pockets bulged with folded bills, and I had to be careful each time I reached in and yanked money out to give change so that the bills wouldn't fly away in a warm and gritty Midwestern wind that was as familiar to me as snow in winter.

At our peak, I would personally profit anywhere from five hundred dollars to a thousand dollars for a single weekend of work. I would take my money to the mall during the week and burn through it all, mostly on albums and clothes. A cute girl with dark hair worked at J&R Music World, and I had hoped buying the entire back catalog of a band like the Police would impress her, so I would show up several times a week, carrying a pile of albums to the register for her to ring up. I would wear new clothes I'd bought at Chess King, maybe even a skinny tie like the kind Billy Joel wore at the time. But the girl, who was a few years older than me, was not impressed—not by my money, not by my musical tastes, and not by my clothes. Not by anything I did or said. Nothing worked. Nothing.

●

Here's what I knew about Barry: He lived in the small central Illinois town where my father and I had been going the previous five years for their annual festival. He had been a high school teacher but had been fired for reasons he only vaguely alluded to. A fling with several students' mothers who became jealous and vengeful, he told us once. He was in his thirties or forties and was fit, but his looks and my perception of him shifted depending upon who was looking at him—handsome and smiling if others were around, sinister and hungry if the only eye he had caught was mine. For reasons I couldn't at first fathom, he had befriended my father.

I didn't like Barry, but I couldn't quite put my finger on it at first. He came behind our table when he talked to us, which I didn't like at all. He stood too close. He met my eyes too often. I was, when I first met him, twelve years old and fat, but by our last encounter, I was sixteen and thin. Ever since I had begun losing weight, Barry would make note of how good I was looking.

"You have a girlfriend?" he'd ask, and when I'd shake my head, he'd say, "No? Why not?" He'd look me up and down, and then he'd meet my eyes again. To my father, he'd say, "You got a lady killer here," and then he'd put his hand on my back and let it linger too long.

"I don't like him," I told my father on several occasions.

"Why?"

"I don't like the way he looks at me."

"What the hell does that mean?"

And then I'd shake my head. My father had a blind spot whenever it came to men who gave him the least bit of their time. He was flattered. It stroked his ego. It didn't make a difference who they were or the nature of their character. If they gave him their ear, my father would in turn give them the benefit of the doubt.

"You know what?" he'd say. "You and your mother are just alike. Suspicious of everyone."

No, I thought. Only those worthy of suspicion.

The last year we went to Barry's town—the year I was sixteen—I had decided around lunchtime that I needed a break from my father, so I walked to the McDonald's near the highway, several miles away. I walked for well over an hour, mostly on gravel roads with cornfields on either side of me. I walked until the road grew wider and turned from gravel to pavement. It was July, hotter than shit, but I didn't care. I listened to my Walkman all the way there, an Elton John cassette I had made for myself, an unofficial "best of." I walked and walked until I finally saw the golden arches.

I ordered my usual—a quarter pounder with cheese, a large fry, a Diet Coke, and a deep-fried apple pie—and then I sat down and took my sweet-ass time eating it. Being alone, eating my favorite food: this was bliss. I wanted to stay all day, but I couldn't. I knew my father was going to be pissed that I had been gone for so long, but so be it. I couldn't take it anymore—the same subjects, over and over, year after year, followed by, "What do you think?" My father hated whenever I was gone longer than he thought I should be gone, if only because he had to stand behind the table in silence. Not that he'd admit that this was the reason. But I knew. And so I braced myself when our table came back into view. What I didn't expect was for Barry, who looked panicked, to be standing there beside my father.

"I drove all over looking for you," Barry said. "I'd have given you a ride."

"Where the hell have you been?" my father asked.

"McDonald's," I said.

"I checked McDonald's," Barry said. "I drove over there. Which way did you go?"

"I don't know," I said. "I walked past a lot of cornfields."

Barry looked confused. Then his eyes widened. "You walked to the highway?"

I nodded. Why was Barry even asking questions? Why was this of any concern to him?

Barry turned to my father. "That's four or five miles each way," he said. To me, he said, "You all right? You need some water?"

"I'm fine," I said.

I looked at my father, hoping he could see now how wrong this all was, but my father was still fuming about how long I had been gone. I turned back to Barry, who looked as though he'd missed his one opportunity to be alone with me, and he must have realized by the look I was giving him that it was too late now. I was onto him.

"We were worried about you," Barry said, but when he reached for my arm, I backed away. Even if my father couldn't see it, I knew that I had just avoided something awkward at best and dangerous at worst. And Barry knew I knew.

He walked around to the other side of the table and I never saw him again, but what disturbed me more was the fact that my father couldn't see what was so obviously wrong, how I was the one he was upset with and not this stranger whose own sketchy backstory didn't add up. For the rest of his life, I could never reconcile my father's blind willingness to trust a stranger over the more rational opinions of those closest to him.

•

As with most profitable enterprises, a rift occurred in the upper management. My father and I had been partners for eleven years at this point, nearly all of my life, and we had weathered several bad years with little profit, but now, finally, we were enjoying the fruits of our labor. Or we should have been, at least.

The problem was this. My father had taken to telling anyone who would listen that the idea to sell T-shirts had been his. "This was the best goddamn idea I ever had," he'd say.

The idea, of course, had been mine. I remembered clearly the idea coming to me during one of my high school classes after months of seeing my classmates wearing different black concert T-shirts day after day. These shirts were all some of my classmates ever wore. Sabbath.

Rush. Zeppelin. The very day the idea came to me that this was what we should be selling, I told my father.

I was used to my father's revisionist histories, but I wasn't going to let him take credit for a suggestion that was now making us thousands of dollars each week. I couldn't let it slide.

And so I brought it up to my mother, who brought it up to my father, who denied that it had been my idea. He laughed it off.

"No, no," he said. "I remember when the idea came to me."

"What?" I yelled. "Are you kidding?"

"Hey! Watch your tone," my father said.

"But it was *my* idea," I said, a whine creeping into my voice.

My father yelled, "What the hell difference does it make?"

"What difference? You're telling everyone it was *your* idea. That's what difference it makes."

"Well," he said, getting angrier. "It *was* my idea."

I knew my father wasn't going to concede, so I left the house, my fists balled up, strange animal noises escaping from my throat. "*Gotttamnnnnitarghhhhhhhh.*" What I wanted was for my father to admit that all of his ideas had resulted in failure while my one idea, my only idea, was making us a small fortune, but I knew the man well enough to know that he had convinced himself that the idea really had been his. The memory of our conversation when I brought the idea to him? It was gone. Long fucking gone. Lost in the vast ocean of his own words and the sound of his own voice.

•

Around this time, we started seeing some competition. The competition, who were people we knew from the circuit who stole our idea, cut our profits in half. My father began driving us farther and farther away to escape the competition, which meant less sleep for me and longer monologues from my father.

Early one morning, while I was setting up a table, a young woman approached our table. She was holding her daughter's hand. The girl couldn't have been older than three. The top of her head barely reached the lip of the table. I was working alone. My father was busy chatting up one of the other sellers, probably buying whatever tall tale the seller was telling him. My father liked to believe that the other flea marketers were making lucrative livings by driving across the country in RVs and selling their shitty things. My father was gullible that way. If the subject was money, he believed whatever preposterous story anyone told him.

The mother standing at my table was pretty, and when she smiled at me, I smiled back. She stopped at the AC/DC T-shirt and read it aloud to her daughter.

"See what this says?" she said. "It says 'Highway to Hell.' And that's exactly where that man is going for selling these," she said, nodding toward me. "He's going to hell when he dies."

My hands began to shake. I was so angry, I felt like vomiting. I said, "If you're not going to buy anything, just move along."

Before walking away, she smiled at me in that self-satisfied way, as though to say, See? You're not a nice boy at all. And in that moment I wasn't a nice boy because I wanted to lean across the table and punch that woman. I wanted to knock that goddamn smile off her face.

It was that precise moment when I realized that I was done. I was done listening to people tell me that I was going to hell for selling stupid T-shirts. I was done listening to my father's monologues that went on for hours and hours. I was done waking up at ungodly hours, only to spend my weekends doing something I truly hated. The money was great, but the satisfaction of knowing it was over was greater. I felt relieved, much as I would feel relieved years later leaving other unpleasant jobs. The money wasn't enough. I hated what I was doing, but I hadn't realized just how much I hated it until I decided never to do it again.

I was so happy, I wanted to weep.

•

Not only did I never sell another thing at a flea market or town festival after that day, I didn't even go to a flea market or town festival for another twenty years. I would, of course, hold down any number of other jobs for periods as long as several years and as short as a day— movie theater usher, delivery man, shipping and receiving attendant, mall greeter, standardized test scorer, dormitory resident assistant. I even regularly sold plasma to make money. I did freelance writing and editing jobs. I threw parties and charged a cover. I did whatever I needed to do to stay afloat. And I also put myself in debt. Student loans. Credit cards. Personal loans. I couldn't dig myself out. I was in too deep. And so I worked, sometimes as many as three jobs at once: a full-time job, a part-time job at night, and temp work on the weekends. And even then I mostly managed just to scrape by.

Eleven years after I quit working with my father, I was a student in a PhD program in English, and my father had driven to Nebraska to visit me. My father never gave a time frame for how long his visits would last, and if I asked him, he would act as though he'd been insulted and leave, so his visits were always pressure cookers of tension and anxiety.

One afternoon, about a week into my father's visit, I had come home from a particularly frustrating day of teaching, and as soon as I stepped inside my suffocatingly small apartment, my father said, "How was your day?"

Instead of giving him a broad overview, I started talking about the fact that so few of my students could punctuate dialogue.

"Instead of putting the comma inside the quotation mark," I said, "they put it outside. Or they don't put one in at all. Or . . ."

My father stopped me. He said, "Why do you think I care about this? I'm not a writer. I don't know what the hell you're talking about."

And that was the moment. The pressure cooker exploded.

I said, "I don't expect you to know about this or care about it, but why the fuck do you think I'd have cared about anything you talked about all those years when we drove to flea markets? Why would a ten-year-old give a shit about measurements for boards you were going to cut or the truck you were going to buy or the sizes of engines or any of the shit you talked about? But did I ever say to you 'I don't care about this'? No! You know why? Because I was polite. But you know what? I didn't give a shit. About any of it! So the least you could have done was listen to me bitch about commas for ten fucking minutes."

As soon as I was done I realized I had stabbed my father through the heart and there was no taking it back. He was sixty-one that year, but he looked older as he sat there looking down into his cup of coffee. He didn't have any money. His clothes were from Goodwill. All those years of work had amounted to nothing. What I had said was cruel, but it was too late to take any of it back.

"I'm sorry," he said, and though it wouldn't be the last time, it was the first time I remembered him apologizing to me for anything.

I sat down across from him that day in Nebraska. Whatever story he had told himself about the two of us, whatever grand and thrilling adventures he had remembered us having together, I had shattered it. And there was no putting it back together.

"Okay," I said to fill the void. "Okay."

•

My father died at eighty years old with only a few hundred dollars in his checking account, and he'd had that much only because he hadn't paid his bills before he died. He didn't have any belongings worth any money, and there was no savings account. His credit was shot. Up until the very end, he'd say to me, whenever we spoke on the phone, "Boy, I'd love to see you hit it big one day. Wouldn't that be something!" Instead of filling me with optimism, my father's hope for me always made me despair.

I'm fifty-one years old as I write this. Twice divorced. Four cats. No kids. I live in Louisiana but have a house in North Carolina that I can't sell. And student loans. Good lord, those student loans. Each month, the credit card bills come with balances slightly larger than the previous month's. But I have projects in the works—a few big ones that could turn my ledger from red to black, if only they'd come through.

I'm a tenured professor. I consider supplementing my income by driving for Uber or selling my collection of first editions or opening up an account on eBay for selling everything in my home. But the truth is, I'm tired—too tired to embark on yet another money-making venture.

My father's idea of the American dream was to make a killing. To be rich. My idea? To live in a small apartment in the city of my choice. To own nothing but a few of my favorite books, a handful of the albums I most love, an adequate stereo to listen to them on, and a comfortable chair. To owe nobody anything. Not one goddamn thing. To die debt free. That's the dream.

THE HIPPEST TRIP IN BURBANK

To my knowledge, not a single black person lived in my southwest Chicago suburb while I was growing up there. Not one. Not in the 1970s, not in the early 1980s. There were a lot of immigrants—Polish, Italian, Greek—and there were a few kids whose parents had come from Mexico. Hell, I was even friends with a Saudi Arabian boy, the only Muslim I knew back then, but I didn't know a single black person.

This isn't to say that I had never seen or talked to black people. There were black people at the mall and in downtown Chicago and on Maxwell Street, where my father took me once a year to buy me a new coat, but you would not have seen a black person waiting for a bus in Burbank, and it was the rare occasion when you would see a black person driving a car down Seventy-Ninth Street, which bisects the city. This wasn't unusual for the Chicago area, where an overpass might divide two neighborhoods by ethnicity, and where it was well advised to stay on your own side of the road. It was as though someone had posted a sign: WELCOME TO BURBANK. BLACK PEOPLE NOT WELCOME. But there was no sign. There didn't need to be one. Somehow, through means I didn't understand, this fact was known.

•

Mariah worked with my mother at the Mead factory, which produced corrugated boxes. She and my mother, working side by side on the assembly line and taking smoke breaks together, developed a friendship, and my mother wanted to have her over for dinner. The issue for my mother was never what our neighbors might think. The issue was Mariah's safety. Mariah was black.

"If I want to have a friend over," my mother said one evening, "then I should be able to have over whoever I want."

My father, who jumped at opportunities to be cavalier, said, "Then have her over."

And so it was settled.

•

My father saw himself as racially progressive, and by and large, given the limitations of his background (he was a high school dropout with a lower-class, rural upbringing), he *was* racially progressive. But he always wanted to make the point of his progressiveness by telling this story.

In 1957, he and my mother drove from Chicago to Hernando, Mississippi, to get married after their third date. My mother had grown up in Tennessee; my father was from Maine. My mother's younger brother, Buddy, went along to be their witness.

At the courthouse, my father bent down to use the water fountain when he heard Buddy frantically yell, "Bob! What're you doing? You can't use that one!" My father looked up, saw a sign that said "Coloreds," and asked, "Is the water any different?" Buddy said, "Well, no," and my father said, "Okay then," and used the fountain.

For my father, there needed to be no more proof than this anecdote, which he wore like a badge, to show that he treated all people equally, regardless of race. But of course this anecdote has nothing to do with being racially progressive and everything to do with my father puffing himself up to make a point, as I would see him do time and again. In all fairness to my father, I would see many white people do this throughout my life, especially in academia, where puffing oneself up is as automatic and as natural as breathing. My father wasn't unique in this regard.

•

But I suppose when it comes to race we all wear our anecdotes like badges.

My badge used to be how much black pop culture I embraced as a kid, but truth be told I'm not sure how much of a role race actually played. I was a fat kid, so I identified with Fat Albert. I grew up living mostly in crappy apartment buildings, so I felt a kinship with Jimmy J. J. Walker on *Good Times*, whose character lived in a crappy housing project in Chicago. Like the son in *Sanford and Son*, I sold antiques with my father (not really antiques . . . just old junk), albeit at flea markets and not out of our home, and also like the son, I often felt anxious and embarrassed by my father's abrasive personality. I took martial arts classes, so Black Belt Jones was one of my heroes. I wanted to be a famous child singer, and so little Michael Jackson from nearby Gary, Indiana, who was only a few years older than me, was a role model. I was keenly aware that all of these celebrities (or cartoon characters, in the case of Fat Albert and his friends) were black, but in truth I gravitated to just as many, if not more, white celebrities.

When I was in the seventh grade, the landmark miniseries *Roots* brought the realities of slavery to prime time. Like millions of other viewers, I was gripped by the show and horrified by the realities of slavery, about which I had known little beyond the broad strokes. But once the series ended, I didn't dive into more research about slavery. Instead, I bought a book with a gold-embossed tree on its cover so that I could piece together my own family tree. How exciting! What lurid tales might my own ancestors have been a party to? Oh, I wrote a fan letter to Ben Vereen, the African American actor who played Chicken George in *Roots*, and he sent back an autographed photo, which I hung up in my room, but I wrote to Jimmy Stewart, Jerry Lewis, and Johnny Carson, too. It was celebrity that I was enamored by, not specifically African American celebrities. Race had nothing to do with it.

Perhaps my single most honest appreciation of black culture came in the form of *Soul Train*, but I had come to *Soul Train* slowly. Like pretty much every other white kid in America, I was weaned on the bland, very pale *American Bandstand*. *Soul Train* followed *American Bandstand*, and even though the formats of the two shows were similar, I considered *Soul Train* taboo. No one had told me not to watch it; I just didn't know anyone who did. In May 1975, when I was nine, Elton John appeared on *Soul Train* to perform "Bennie and the Jets" and "Philadelphia Freedom," and I watched the show for the first time.

I watched because I was an Elton John fan, but while listening to the other songs that played before and after Elton's two performances, I realized that this was same music I was already listening to, music I had been listening to for years. I owned records by Gladys Knight at the Pips, the Jackson 5, and the Isley Brothers. Furthermore, the dancing on *Soul Train* was *way* more exciting than the dancing on *American Bandstand*, which was passionless, chaste. And Don Cornelius was so much cooler than Dick Clark. *Soul Train* had it all: the opening credits in which a cartoon train weaves its way through urban tenements like those in Chicago, where the show was born; funky neon letters that spelled *Soul Train*; and the famous Soul Train Line where individual dancers had a brief moment in the spotlight to showcase their best moves while dancing between two rows of men and women who waited their turn. And the clothes! Oh, hell yeah, I wanted to dress like the dancers on *Soul Train*. Huge collars and platform shoes and bell-bottom pants with sequins. The other shows I watched were endorsed by companies that made things our family used, but I had never seen Ultra Sheen or Afro Sheen in our house. In fact, I had never seen these products in the stores we shopped at, either. This was a new world for me, and I loved everything about it. *Soul Train* was, as it called itself, the hippest trip in America, and I truly wanted to hop on that train and take that ride, even if I was to be the only white boy onboard.

•

My mother had a story, too, but my mother was a natural storyteller, and the point of telling it wasn't to present a moral lesson or to pat herself on the back, the way it was for my father. If anything, like all good stories, my mother's story was local, which is to say, it was about family and the brutality within. And like all good stories, it had a subtext—in this case, one that was rooted in the South's dark and troubled past.

My mother had grown up in a sharecropping family; she began picking cotton at the age of three. Her father had had several children with his first wife, and when that wife died, he married her younger sister, with whom he fathered five more children. The youngest children were twins, a boy and a girl. My mother was the next youngest.

Her father's name was Charlie Triplett. A wiry man with ropy arms, Charlie drank too much and was prone to violence, and my mother feared him, even though she was his favorite. On more than one occasion, she had seen him violently beat one or another of her siblings.

This was rural Tennessee, 1942. One day, when my mother was eight, she walked to the country store with her older brother Pete and older half-sister Geneva. Pete and Geneva were probably thirteen and fifteen. Inside the store were an older black man and an older black woman, husband and wife, and when the man saw my mother, he grinned and said, "Are you one of Charlie Triplett's girls?"

"Yes, sir," my mother said.

The man said, "Why, I knew it. I can tell by your face."

The woman said, "You've got pretty hair."

My mother, who was not fond of her curly, nearly orange hair, said, "Thank you, ma'am."

"You tell your father Hawkins said hello," the man said.

"I will, sir," she said.

The woman said, "You have a good day now."

"Thank you, ma'am. You, too," my mother said.

On their way home, Pete said, "You're gonna get in trouble, girl."

"Why?" my mother asked.

Geneva said, "You don't call niggers *sir* and *ma'am*. Wait 'til Daddy hears what you did."

My mother began crying, but Geneva and Pete wouldn't let up. They said, "Daddy's gonna give you a whipping, girl!" And: "You won't be able to sit for a week."

My mother remembered other whippings her father had given, like the time one of her older brothers, who was fighting in the war, had forgotten one of her older sister's birthdays. When that sister said, "I hope he dies over there," her father beat her until she couldn't move.

My mother feared the same fate: a beating that would leave her motionless on the floor. Why, she wondered, had she called the old man *sir*? Why had she called the old woman *ma'am*? Why hadn't she just kept her mouth shut?

She begged her brother and sister not to tell on her, but the knowledge they possessed made them powerful, gleeful. How could they *not* tell?

•

My mother knew that inviting Mariah, her friend and coworker, over for dinner wouldn't be as easy as, well, simply inviting her. This was 1973 in an all-white Chicago suburb. Martin Luther King Jr. had been assassinated only five years earlier, prompting riots. Our neighborhood was blue-collar, often violent, and it was not, by any stretch of imagination, what one might have considered progressive.

Once my mother settled on a date for Mariah to come to dinner, she began making preparations. The task was to secure a parking space for Mariah. Since the apartment we lived in had assigned spaces, my father parked one of our vehicles in the space of a friend who worked a late shift. The parking space issue gave us an excuse to meet Mariah outside so that we could guide her into the correct space and then walk her to our building and up into our apartment on the second floor. This way, we could be a makeshift security detail, casually staggered around her, a buffer against danger. But we would try to appear merely as a cheerful gaggle of white people waiting in the parking lot as Mariah pulled her car in, and we would greet her more enthusiastically than we had ever greeted anyone while my father surveyed the area, making sure no trouble was afoot.

•

Most of the time, I wasn't aware that I was being exposed to racism. Nonetheless, I was surrounded by it all the time, either implicitly by the fact that there were no black people living in Burbank or explicitly in the things people said, including those close to me. One of my aunts once said to me, as we drove through a neighborhood where black people lived, "Don't talk. They can read lips, you know."

This nugget of information confused me for years. Why had black people learned to read lips? And why would they care what we were saying? Also, I would have loved to have been able to read lips—I was always trying to figure out what people were saying—so I was envious of these black people who apparently could do so.

Years later, when I was in college, this same aunt gave me a box of books, as assortment of musty Book Club selections. It was, I had thought, a kind gesture, but when I pulled out a novel by Frank Yerby, my aunt said, "He's a nigger writer, but he's pretty good."

By then, I had been away from Burbank for a number of years. I had escaped to a different world, a more appealing world, and her words sucked the air from my lungs. I sat there, dazed. Had she just said what I thought she had said? She was an old woman who had lost both legs to diabetes, and there was nothing I was going to say at this late date to change her way of thinking. I silently put the books back into the box, thanked her, and carried them out to my car.

•

When I was a kid, I absorbed everything having to do with humor, whether it was watching silent Charlie Chaplin or Our Gang films, memorizing vaudeville routines, reading books about Abbott and Costello, or listening to comedy albums like Cheech and Chong's or George Carlin's, whose "Seven Words You Can't Say on Television" I would merrily recite to my classmates. Looming over all of these comedians, however, was Richard Pryor.

I had discovered Richard Pryor through his guest appearances on TV, which led me in 1974 to buy his album (in 8-track tape format) *That Nigger's Crazy*. I was nine years old. My parents rarely censored what I watched, listened to, or bought. My mother probably thought Pryor swore too much, but both she and my father would listen to my comedy albums along with me, and *That Nigger's Crazy* was no exception. The album originally appeared on one of Stax's labels, and it was recorded in Don Cornelius's Soul Train nightclub. It won a Grammy for best comedy album, marking the beginning of Pryor's meteoric rise.

Pryor's comedy often dealt with race, and it had the effect of making me, at a young age, sympathetic to, while also informing me of, the plight of black people. Even when he hosted *Saturday Night Live* in December 1975, race dominated his comedy. Perhaps his most famous sketch was when he interviews for a job with Chevy Chase, who conducts the interview. Chase asks Pryor to say the first word that pops into his head in a word association test. As Chase's words turn into racial insults, Pryor, whose eyes widen and whose anger comes to a full boil, matches him insult for insult.

Chase: "Jungle bunny."

Pryor: "Honky!"

Chase: "Spade."

Pryor: "Honky, honky!"

Chase: "Nigger."

Pryor: "*Dead* honky!"

There weren't many *Saturday Night Live* reruns back in 1975 when this first aired, but I owned an album of *Saturday Night Live's* greatest hits, and this skit was on it. I wore out the grooves from playing it over and over and memorizing it, same as I had memorized Steve Martin's routines or Abbott and Costello's "Who's on First?"

•

For Mariah's visit, my mother served her homemade spaghetti and meatballs, and then my parents and Mariah smoked and talked until the apartment was foggy. I likely showed her my Evel Knievel toys, but to be honest, I remember few specific details about that night, all the rest of it denouement to the invitation, preparation, and safe arrival into our home. What I do remember was my hyper-awareness of what we were doing by inviting Mariah into our home, and now here she was among us, eating and smoking and talking.

We never had Mariah over again after that night, but this wouldn't have been unusual. What was unusual was that we'd had a guest over—*any* guest—who was not a relative or someone who lived in our building. We were an insular family in that regard. We kept to ourselves.

After Mariah's visit, I never saw another black person in Burbank while I lived there—not on foot, not in a car, and certainly not in anyone's house. Mariah would be the first and last, for all that I knew.

•

A turning point for Richard Pryor came when he began starring in movies, most notably teaming up with Gene Wilder, the first pairing of which was in the movie *Silver Streak*. Race occasionally played a role in the movies, but unlike his albums and stand-up routines, the issue of race was made into palatable comedy for white America.

Silver Streak is a comedy-thriller about a murder on a train. The movie was released in winter 1976 when I was in sixth grade, and my parents took me to see it. I loved it, of course. But there was one scene in particular that I loved—that everyone in the theater loved, in fact. In this scene, Gene Wilder needs to walk undetected by the police, and Richard Pryor convinces him to pass for black by wearing shoe polish on his face and wearing Richard Pryor's clothes, which includes a shiny purple jacket. While Wilder smears the black shoe polish across his face, he listens to some funk music on the radio and tries "acting" black. Wilder, however, is painfully white in his movements. When he exits the public bathroom, Pryor cringes because of how horrifically exaggerated Wilder appears in his attempt to pass. Our sympathies in this scene are with Pryor's character.

During this same time, I had become a student of comedy, working on my own book about old-time comedians while continuing to work on my own repertoire of stolen comedy routines. In little over a year, I would win second place in a talent competition with my stolen Steve Martin stand-up act. But in the meantime—specifically, in

October 1977—I had a flash of inspiration that I mistook for genius. For Halloween, I would go as Gene Wilder. But not Gene Wilder in general. I would go as Gene Wilder in the scene that had earned him the loudest laugh in *Silver Streak*: the scene where he puts on black shoe polish and tries to pass for black.

It was an unusually complicated costume in concept but not in execution. For some now-unfathomable reason, I was positive that everyone would understand the concept upon sight. But of course I offered no context for the concept. I was eleven years old; I was in seventh grade. *Context* wasn't in my vocabulary.

The way things usually worked on Halloween was that kids would go home for lunch, put on their costumes, and then return to reap the rewards of having strapped on a Snoopy or Charlie Brown mask. Nearly all of the costumes were store-bought and, in my humble opinion, lame. There was no imagination; there was nothing groundbreaking.

My brother, who was older and had been in high school plays, would likely have had the necessary greasepaint. He also went to discos with names like the Poison Apple and owned a shiny jacket I would need as well, which would surely leave no doubt that my costume was Gene Wilder in that specific scene in *Silver Streak*. When I was in the third grade, someone had given my mother, who was a redhead, a curly black wig. In other words, I had everything I needed.

When I stepped out of the bathroom and my mother saw me covered in black greasepaint and wearing her black wig, she said, "Johnny. What are you supposed to be?"

I said, "I'm Gene Wilder in *Silver Streak*."

My mother was sitting at the dining room table. She had a cup of coffee in one hand and a cigarette in the other. She set the coffee cup down and said, "I don't think that's a good idea."

"What?"

"Dressing up like that," she said. "Pretending to be black. It's not right."

"I'm not pretending to be *black*. I'm dressed as *Gene Wilder*, who pretends to be black."

My mother said, "No one's going to see it that way."

I said, "What do you mean? That was the funniest part of the movie."

My mother took a long drag off her cigarette and said, "You're not going to school like that."

"Yes I am," I said. "This is my costume."

"Why don't you just go as a monster?"

"Because," I said, "everyone's a monster. Or Snoopy. Or something stupid. No one's ever done this before."

I should say this about my mother: She wasn't afraid to let me fail. But it was also clear that whenever I ignored her opinion, which was rare, I would be on my own. Completely and utterly on my own. My mother sighed and said, "Okay. You better hurry then so you're not late."

I waited for her to stand up and pick up her purse. I waited, but she was not moving from her seat.

"You're not driving me?" I finally asked.

My mother shook her head. "Nope. I don't want anyone to see me with you," she said.

My own mother was abandoning me?

"Okay then," I said. "Fine."

Wearing a black wig and black gloves, I lit out for school with black greasepaint covering my face and neck. My school was only six blocks away, but the further from home I walked, the heavier the weight of what I'd done to myself became. Cars slowed down so that drivers could get a better look.

Did they think that I was a black person? I began to sweat now. I considered jogging the rest of the way, but would that draw even more attention to me?

At school, as I neared the blacktop where kids would already be lining up to go inside, I paused to catch my breath. What in the world had I been thinking? Why hadn't I listened to my mother? She was almost always right. Why had I ignored her on what now seemed a catastrophic decision?

When I rounded the corner and saw yet another grave error, it was all I could do not to start weeping. All the younger kids had dressed up for Halloween, but none of the seventh and eighth grade kids. Clearly, I had missed an important announcement.

My classmates were about to enter the school in a single-file line for the second half of the day. After finding an unlocked door and slipping inside the junior high wing, I ran to the bathroom and, using industrial paper towels, wiped off the grease paint as best as I could. I had to use my shirt in order to remove most of it. I stuffed my mother's wig in a front pocket, my gloves in another. I splashed water onto my face several times, but no matter how many times I did this, black greasepaint remained visible somewhere on my skin. Since I didn't want to call special attention to myself by showing up late to class, I left the bathroom, slipped in line, and joined my classmates as we trudged to our respective homerooms.

The students who sat nearest stared hard at me. "What's that on your neck?" one of them asked.

"Dirt."

"It doesn't look like dirt. It looks like . . . makeup."

"It's dirt," I repeated. "Now shut up."

Another boy told me I looked awful.

"So do you," I said.

More than one teacher gave me the once-over but didn't say anything.

After school, I ran home, wig and gloves still crammed inside my pockets.

My mother, sitting in a recliner and smoking, said, "Well? How did it go?"

"You were right," I said. "It wasn't a good idea."

My mother never rubbed it in on the few occasions I had foolishly ignored her advice, but she also wasn't one to try to make me feel better for having not taken her advice. I *should* have taken her advice, after all. This occasion was no different. She raised her eyebrows ever so slightly. This was her way of saying, Mm-hm . . . *I see.* And then we never broached the subject again.

•

Years later, while teaching a freshman composition class at an elite private university populated mostly with wealthy, conservative white kids, we were discussing an essay about the importance of diversity on campus when a student raised her hand and proclaimed that she had chosen that particular university because everyone there looked like her. "The campus visit . . . it made me feel at home," she said. The sole black student in that class—a football player—was absent that day. The remainder of the students were white. When another arm shot up, I hoped it was to counter the young woman's view, but, as I should have guessed, it was to add support. With the exception of only one student, every student who participated in the conversation was saying (without actually coming right out and saying it) that they had chosen this school because there weren't many black students, which prompted from me a long, didactic anecdote with the hope of illuminating why they were wrongheaded. Even as I spoke, I saw the light fade from their eyes, a light that had only moments earlier glowed at the communal pride of being able to say what they had all secretly felt but hadn't, until then, publicly admitted. And then came the sad realization that I was not one of them. I was one of *those.* I was a liberal.

But here's what I've come to realize—that as an eleven-year-old boy I would not have shown up at my school wearing blackface if there had been even one black student or black teacher. I felt safe in the community of white people. The worst that would have happened was that I would have been ridiculed. That was my license as a white boy.

•

After their trip to the grocery store, after their walk through the woods, my mother's brother and sister told their father what my mother had done, that she had called a couple of niggers "sir" and "ma'am." They told the whole story to Charlie Triplett. The house was so small, a sharecroppers' house, that there was no place for my mother to hide. After Pete and Geneva told what my mother had done, Charlie stood up and walked over to my mother.

"Is this true?"

My mother nodded.

"You called them *sir* and *ma'am*?"

My mother nodded again.

"And what about you two?" Charlie asked Pete and Geneva. "What did you call them when they talked to you?"

Pete said, "We don't talk to niggers."

Charlie nodded. He removed his belt. Walking over to Pete and Geneva, he said, "You always call people older than you *ma'am* and *sir*, you hear me?"

Geneva knew better than to speak, but Pete said, "But they were niggers."

Charlie said nothing more. According to my mother, Charlie Triplett beat both Pete and Geneva so hard that she thought he was going to kill them. When he had finished whipping them, he put the belt back through its loops and said, "How do you think it makes me look when my own kids don't treat their elders with respect?"

My mother told me this story often, but she told several stories often, many of them with more ambiguous or mysterious outcomes, usually of the Southern gothic variety, like the one about the woman who gave birth to babies two months apart, or the one about the conjoined twins who lived in a cabin in the woods. The story about the older black couple was yet another story, except that this one took place in the South in the 1940s, and there were black people in it who were old enough to have been born into slavery, but it was a story nonetheless, one with a beginning, middle, and an end.

•

Until now I had told only two people about what I did that Halloween all those years ago. I had told both of my ex-wives but no one else. I can count on one hand the stories from my life that I can't say aloud, and this is one of them. Yes, it was forty years ago; yes, I was eleven years old. But neither fact matters. I wonder sometimes if I added the context of the movie later to excuse what I had done. If you tell yourself a lie long enough, you eventually believe the lie. I don't think I made it up to excuse what would have been behavior even more difficult to forgive, but I can't say for certain that I didn't, just as I can't tell you what the weather was like that day, nor do I remember the make and model of any of the cars whose drivers slowed down to look at me. All I know for certain is what I did and how I feel about it now.

•

I have no end to this story. Nor do I have a moral. The harder I search for an epiphany, the more it eludes me. I left Burbank at the age of seventeen. I have since had black classmates in college, black colleagues, black friends, black neighbors, a black girlfriend. I teach black authors and have muddled my way through many class discussions on race. I offer these facts not as badges of honor, only as facts of things that would likely not have existed in my life if I had stayed in Burbank.

My mother and Mariah are no longer alive. They both died many years ago of cancer. But I often think of that dinner invitation and wonder what Mariah must have thought when she pulled into the parking lot and saw the four of us standing there, waiting. We must have looked like the kind of happy white family you'd see on TV—all four of us grinning and waving her into a parking space, receiving the only black person we had ever seen in Burbank.

Hello, hello, hello, hello!
Welcome, welcome, welcome, welcome!

Surely Mariah knew the risk she was taking. Parking her car, getting out, and hugging my mother—those were acts of courage. I wouldn't have blamed her if she had kept on driving.

PART TWO
The Fat Boy's Fat Body

IN THE FIELD BEHIND THE CONDO WHERE THE FAT BOY PLAYS

In the summer of 1975, my parents finally became homeowners when they bought a condominium unit in Burbank in a brand-new development comprised of eight buildings. The cost: $25,000. First, however, we had to break our apartment lease and move out in the middle of the night. I was nine years old, carrying my toys down the stairs to my father's pickup at three in the morning while everyone else, our friends and enemies, slept soundly. In every apartment building we'd ever lived, we always had friends and we always had enemies, and we never lived in any one place for longer than two years. Things were finally going to be different.

Once settled in the condo, I started a dog-walking business, and before long I was walking, along with my dog Shoo Shoo, two neighbor dogs: Moo and Ralph. Behind the eight buildings was a large field of weeds intermittently dotted by trees. The field extended all the way back to an electric fence, and beyond that fence was an industrial park. I rarely walked that far, fearful of running across kissing teenagers and grade school ruffians on minibikes. Also back there was Dead Man's Pond, a small body of toxic water around which teenagers drank beer and smoked pot. Fat and nine years old, I would not have been a welcome sight.

From that field behind the condos, I could see the Sears Tower downtown and, farther behind it, like a shorter sibling, the John Hancock Building, but that was as much of the city's skyline as I could make out. Frequently, a Goodyear blimp floated over the field behind the condominiums, and while the three dogs sniffed trees or each other, I would recite what I remembered of the radio broadcast of the

Hindenburg explosion: "Oh, the humanity! This is the worst thing I've ever witnessed!" Midway airport, only a few miles north, was a ghost town, but occasionally planes would land there, and each time one descended, I would imagine it crashing just beyond the distant tree line behind which it disappeared. "Puh-*kuhhhhh!*" I would say, imitating the explosion.

Standing in that field, holding the dogs' leashes, I pretended to be other people—a disc jockey introducing songs like "Dream Weaver" and "Someone Saved My Life Tonight"; a rock star singing a song I'd made up, the monotonous (but in my imaginary world enormously popular) "Money Hunger"; a vaudevillian whose audience for "Who's on First?" was a trio of panting mutts. I also tortured insects in that field. I did horrible, unspeakable things to insects, something I don't like to think about even now, but they were not the only things I tortured. There was a tree behind the condos, tall and healthy, shaped like an upside-down wishbone. I beat one side of that wishbone-shaped tree with whatever I was holding. Usually, I hit it with my keys, which were tied to a shoestring, but I would sometimes pick up a fallen tree limb, often from the very tree I was going to beat, and I would strike it with that limb.

I was a fat kid. I was a fat kid who liked to raise the lids of Dumpsters and peer inside. I was a fat kid who liked to peer inside Dumpsters while tending to three dogs who, in turn, sniffed and licked the Dumpster's delicious wheels. I looked for turntables or old radios with glass vacuum tubes. One time I found a stack of albums. *Woodstock. The Concert for Bangladesh. Yessongs.* Who would throw these out? An angry lover? I reached in, quickly retrieved them, and ran back to our condo, pulling the dogs behind me. Another time, on a day when the dogs weren't with me, I spotted something potentially interesting at the bottom of the Dumpster and, after hoisting myself up onto the diseased lip, tried to tilt so that I could reach in and grab it, but once I started tipping inside, I realized that I was going to fall all the way in. I remained teetering for a good while, imagining distant laughter, before finally giving in and crashing to the bottom, landing on top of two bloated bags of stinking garbage.

Year after year, I tortured insects, beat that tree, sang songs I'd made up, and rooted around the communal Dumpster. The dogs grew old and gray while I grew tall and thin. One day, fourteen years old and no longer a fat boy, I stood hitting the tree with one of its fallen limbs, as I'd done a thousand times before. By then, I had quit torturing insects or picking through Dumpsters, but I still walked dogs and clubbed that tree. I clubbed that tree as though it were the older boy who'd called me fat ass or the adult working on his shitty car who snickered as I, a shy overweight boy on a bicycle, pedaled by. Half the tree was alive but half of it was dead, and still I clubbed that son of a bitch, over and over, until I heard a creaking noise. I didn't realize it was coming from the tree until the tree started to split down the middle. I quickly backed up as the entire tree divided in two, a massive upside-down wishbone pulled apart by invisible giants. The living part remained standing while the dead part crashed to the ground.

I looked behind me to see if anyone had seen what I'd done. I feared retribution. By our fifth year of living in the condo, we had an equal number of friends as we did enemies, and my father tried figuring a way to get us out of there, but we were no longer renters and couldn't slip away in the middle of the night, although I could see in my father's eyes the desire to run, not just away from the condo but away from all of us.

It was too cold for insects that day, and there were no planes in the sky, no blimps floating overhead. I might have felt guilt for what I'd done to the tree or I might have felt nothing. It's in flames now, I might have thought, and the frame is crashing to the ground, not quite to the mooring mast. "Oh, the humanity!" I might have said to the dogs. "This is the worst thing I've ever witnessed." Likely, I returned the dogs to their respective homes and then rode my ten-speed around the neighborhood, pedaling harder and harder, heading both anywhere and nowhere at once. To a stranger glancing up, I would have been an indistinguishable blur on a bicycle, and then I would have been nothing at all. I would have been gone.

THE WILD ONE

Jesus, I rode my bike everywhere. Everywhere! Everywhere, that is, until that day in high school when I stopped to talk to a group of cute girls and racked myself on the bike's bar. But I'm getting ahead of myself.

Bikes, man. First movie I saw at the drive-in? *Easy Rider*. I was three. I probably owned a tricycle, but I don't remember. Tricycles don't count. I'm talking bicycles. Two wheels, motherfucker. Not three. Not four. Not one, for all you unicycle weirdos out there. Two!

Before I even knew who Evel Knievel was, before Evel Knievel had entered the public consciousness, I was rough on bikes. By rough, I mean I used to break them in half. For real. The handlebars are connected to something called the head tube. The head tube is connected to the top tube and the down tube. Most of my bikes broke where the head tube was connected to both the top and down tubes. Are you following? The bike would just break in half. And since I would be holding onto the handlebars, my arms would suddenly be elongated, like Wile E. Coyote's, as the front wheel took off separate from the rest of the bike. Yeah, laugh it up. Hell, I might even have thought it was *fun* for a split second while it was happening until my knees smashed against the concrete, the front wheel continuing to elongate me even though I was lying on the ground. To compound the problem, I was usually wearing shorts and not jeans, so my knees would look like a couple of handfuls of raw hamburger when it was over. I still have scars on my knees. In fact, while I was being put under for knee surgery a few years ago, I overheard someone in the operating room say, "Looks like he already had knee surgery," and I tried saying something like, "Let me explain. Those scars are from when the head tube broke from the top and down tubes from one of my many bicycle accidents way back in the 1970s," but what I likely said, as the anesthetic took hold, was something like, "*Gahhhh* . . . knees! What? Hahahahahahaha," and then passed out.

But I'm getting ahead of myself again.

Bikes.

Bikes, motherfucker. I broke bikes in half. I broke them jumping homemade ramps. I broke them riding down the front steps of an old house that must have had a dozen steps leading up to the front door. I broke them from jumping curbs and doing wheelies and crashing into shit I didn't see, like parked cars. I can't even begin to tell you how many goddamned parked cars I crashed into. Anyone watching me might have thought I wasn't a smart kid. That I was, in point of fact, slow. That I wasn't all there. What they wouldn't have realized was that I was so engrossed in the various mechanics of my bike, in all its peculiar idiosyncrasies, in the delicate intricacies of the stunts I was perfecting, that I just sometimes didn't see the fucking car that was parked in front of me.

I worked on my bikes, too. I modified them. I changed the handlebars. I rotated the tires. One time, after a tire rotation, I forgot to tighten up the bolts on the front tire, and the tire came off while I was soaring down the street. The front wheel rolled off, the forks dug into the street, and I flew over the handlebars. Like Superman. Arms out and everything. I just flew. I mean, holy shit, right? No helmet. And then I landed on my head. *Wham.* This wasn't the only time I flew over handlebars and landed on my head. If I accidentally turned the handlebars too fast, I flew. If my wheel hit a large rock on the road, I flew. I flew if someone threw something at me and, by some statistical improbability, it landed in my spokes, causing everything on my bike to shut down. And I always landed on my head. Always. My head, I have concluded, is as indestructible as a bowling ball. You could detach my head, spend the next twenty years rolling it into a set of pins, and it would remain intact.

I installed a speedometer on one of my bikes. I was the only kid in the neighborhood with a speedometer, but I liked knowing how fast I was going. Five miles an hour, ten miles an hour, twenty miles an hour. I couldn't outrun anyone except for the one fat kid who was fatter than me. But I had strong legs, and I would pump those goddamn pedals. I would stand up on my bike and pump even harder. I would watch the speedometer. I would watch the needle get higher and higher. I would race cars. *You think you're going to go faster than me, asshole? Think again!* Eventually, of course, they would go faster than me. Much faster. Sadly. But so be it.

I must have been a sight to see: a fat boy standing up and pumping those pedals while his belly bounced and buckets of sweat poured down his doughy face. Given how much time I spent on a bike and how hard I pedaled and how fast I went, I don't know why I didn't weigh half of what I did. I was like some early superhuman boy version of Lance Armstrong. Only without the performance-enhancing drugs. Just pure adrenaline. And Ho Hos. That's right. Hostess Ho Hos, bitches.

One of my earliest memories of riding my bike involves getting hit by a car. We were living in this crappy apartment complex in Summit, and just as I was starting to pedal out across the narrow parking lot, a muscle car tore ass around the corner, and I slammed into its front fender. (Technically, I hit the car, the car didn't hit me, but I'm talking legally here.) I don't know how old the driver was. I was five, so anyone older than ten was simply old from my point of view. The driver could have been anywhere between ten and a hundred, but likely he was seventeen or eighteen. He jumped out of his car and started yelling at me. And then he did the last thing you'd ever want to do if a five-year-old on a bike has just hit the front fender of your moving vehicle and suffered a bruised groin. He went to the police station to file a complaint because I had nicked some paint on his car. That's right. The driver of a four-thousand-pound moving vehicle went to the police station to file a complaint against the five-year-old he had (legally, he had thought) hit with his car.

Two police officers stopped by our apartment and asked me to come down to the police station, where I had to show a bunch of strangers my bruised groin. All along, I had assumed I was going to prison. I was five and had seen a lot of movies at the drive-in where innocent people ended up in prison. But then a police officer ushered in the muscle-car-driving pinhead so they could hear his side of the story, and after they listened patiently to it, they explained to him what a shit for brains he was, how the boy he had hit with his ridiculous muscle car had sustained an injury—a bruised groin, no less!—and how I could press charges against him, and how he could lose his license and maybe even go to jail for reckless driving. Would he prefer it that way? Would he like for the boy with the bruised groin to press charges? No? Was he sure? Yes? Okay, then get the fuck out of here and slow the fuck down and don't ever let them see your stupid fucking face again. Understood?

I almost felt sorry for the shit for brains. Almost.

In the fifth grade, I went on a field trip to the Schwinn factory in Chicago to watch bikes being made. And this was, bar none, the best field trip I'd ever been on. No lie. Usually, we'd go to the zoo or a boring theater production or watch some slow-ass turtles at the Shedd Aquarium, but finally—finally!—the school got their shit together and was taking me somewhere I actually wanted to go. Don't get me wrong: I like monkeys and hippos and turtles and what have you, but I could see those on my own time. A factory where bikes were made? Schwinn, no less? Oh, hell, yeah. Years later, when I told this story to a colleague, they started telling me how terrible that was, how clearly I was being indoctrinated to accept factory work as my lot in life, and how they knew what they were doing by taking busloads of kids to a factory at a young age to get us acclimated to the idea. Whenever someone says things like this to me, I usually remain silent. Or crack open an ice-cold Frappuccino and nod meaningfully. Or say something like, "Oh, shit . . . looks like the cats are out of food. Hold on." I mean, sure, Schwinn had their motives. They wanted each of us to go home and ask our parents to buy us brand-new Schwinn bicycles. And that's exactly what I did. And, geniuses that they are at Schwinn, it worked.

And because Schwinns weren't cheap, I had to bargain with my parents, rolling the gift into multiple gifts: It could be my gift for two birthdays, one Christmas, the next four Easters, and any religious activity I had accomplished. The truth was, I never got gifts for Easter or religious crap. Furthermore, my birthday and Christmas were a little over a month apart, and my parents would probably forget by the time my next birthday rolled around. And so we hammered out a deal, and one morning the Schwinn Continental arrived for my bike-riding pleasure. I felt like a pimp on that motherfucker. And, believe me, I knew all about pimps by then. All I needed was a fancy pink hat with a large white feather while I rode my Continental around the neighborhood. My *Schwinn* Continental, that is. A fat boy on his fancy-ass Schwinn.

Did that fat boy just pop a wheelie on that ten-speed?

Mm-hm. Looks that way. Fat boy's got some moves, don't he?

I'd ride around and wave at girls I knew, hoping they'd wave back. I'd ride my bike to the houses of girls I liked and circle their block a dozen times, hoping they'd come out of their houses and say hello and ask to see my bike. I had fantasies about the various doors the new bike would open for me, the new girls I'd meet, the new friends I'd make, but none of these things happened. I remained a lone wolf, riding my bike well into the night, sometimes way beyond where I was supposed to ride my bike, always pushing my limits, the way lone wolves do.

Eventually, I lost weight. And got taller. The summer between the end of grade school and the start of high school, I'd bike to the park where the Little League games took place, and I'd buy ice cream cones for girls I knew. I'd pretend my bike was a motorcycle, the way I'd get on it and off it. The way I'd sit for a good while, gripping the handlebars, before taking off, leaving a plume of dust behind me. I was smooth.

But then high school came, and I rarely rode my bike, choosing instead to walk. I don't know why. Maybe I didn't see any of my peers riding bikes. Maybe it was because I wasn't a fat boy anymore. I was a skinny boy who tried to shed his old fat boy ways. Maybe I had learned that it was easier to attract girls on foot than speeding past them on a five-year-old ten speed and waving. Maybe I had fallen one too many times off the bike. I really don't remember why I suddenly preferred walking. It would be like asking a baby why crawling stopped appealing to them: "At what point did you decide it would be better to stand on your feet than travel by knees?" Who knows why evolution leads us instinctually where it does?

One spring day during my sophomore year of high school, however, I dusted off my bike and got back on it. I was tall and thin, and I wore Jordache designer jeans that highlighted my anatomy in such a way that I might as well have been painted blue from the waist down. I had also reached the pinnacle of craving to be with a girl, any girl, to such an extent that I was always in pain. On that still-cool-but-no-longer-ass-freezing day, I hadn't been on a bike of any kind for quite some time. But there I was, riding it like a pro, standing on the pedals as the bike leaned right and then left and then right and then left, over and over, until I sat back down and let the bike coast, the wind hitting but unable to penetrate the coat of Aqua Net protecting my pompadour. And then I saw a group of girls I knew. I saw them and smiled, and then I squeezed the brakes. That's when it happened. The bike abruptly stopped, I slid off the seat and onto the bar (the top tube, as it were), and I racked my balls. With the exception of a car accident many years later that split open my head, I don't think I've ever experienced as much pain as I felt in that moment. No other bike accident was in the same league. Flying over the handlebars and landing on my bowling ball of a head didn't compare to the unique and exquisite pain that rumbled through me when my now-adult groin slammed against that bar. The very same groin that had been bruised when I had smashed into shit for brain's muscle car all those years earlier. To make matters worse, six girls witnessed the event and then watched as I carefully—oh so carefully—lifted my leg up and over the bike seat and then walked away, not speaking another word.

In the thirty-plus years that followed, I have occasionally ridden bikes but no longer with the gusto or reckless abandon that had once consumed me. I have worn helmets. I have paid attention to cars, both parked and moving. I have obeyed the rules of the road. But, oh, how I still remember the thrill of being airborne, my arms out in front of me. I must have been a thing of beauty: a low-flying fat boy defying gravity and common sense. I always knew that excruciating pain would be in my immediate future, but I chose instead to live in the moment as I soared over the handlebars, flying, flying, flying.

CHUNKYOBDANGLE

I had been a thin, normal-sized kid until second grade.

But then, in the second grade, I stayed with my aunt while my mother was in the hospital and my father was away at work, and my aunt took a vested interest in force-feeding me. She'd prepare lard-based meals that glistened with fat and butter, and then she'd pile it all onto my plate and say, "I'm going to feed you until your eyes pop out." If I started wilting midway through a meal, my uncle—a volatile alcoholic who drowned everything he ate with hot sauce—would say, "Son! You better finish your plate, you hear?"

By the end of my time with my aunt, she had achieved her goal. My clothes were ill-fitting and bursting at the seams, and I was having difficulty keeping up with the other kids during gym class. I wasn't so fat yet as to call attention to myself, but I was well on my way. The die was cast.

•

By fourth grade, I was pretty fat but still not name-calling fat. I was in that range of fat where I could be the class clown, should I have gone that route. In other words, I was jovial fat. I was socially acceptable fat. A fat kid that was still admitted into a group. Not that I belonged to any group, but I wouldn't yet have been shunned from any.

My appetite, however, had multiplied. For breakfast, I would eat three eggs, a pile of bacon, and several pieces of toast with jelly. At McDonald's, I would eat three cheeseburgers, a large fry, an apple pie (the deep-fried kind before McDonald's got all health conscious), and a large Coke. There was no internal mechanism telling me that I was eating too much, so I would simply stuff myself until I couldn't move or until I became too sleepy to keep eating, and then I would finally, mercifully stop.

My unconscious mind, however, knew that my eating and my weight were serious problems, and this unconscious knowledge of myself as a fat boy marks the beginning of my life as a writer. Here's how it happened. My fourth-grade teacher, Ms. Waterman, gave all of us an assignment to write a short play and then act it out. The "acting it out" part scared the hell out of me—I had become a pathologically shy boy—but I threw myself into the "write a short play" part unlike anything I had thrown myself into before.

I found the play's title—Chunkyobdangle—in a seek-and-find book. From there, the play's plot bloomed in its entirety: a fat superhero named Chunkyobdangle goes into a phone booth to change into his superhero costume and gets stuck because he's so fat. It would be a comic play, of course, but for the first time ever, I would be calling attention to the fact that I was fat. By poking fun at myself, I would be making myself vulnerable. At some level, I understood that this was a risk.

I knew it would be easy to make my classmates laugh. The bar was low. I could stand up there and fart for ten minutes, and they'd laugh harder than they'd ever laughed in their lives. But Ms. Waterman? I had no idea what her reaction might be. I saw confusion when I announced the title of the play, but it didn't take long for the laughs to start, and by the time our hero Chunkyobdangle gets stuck in the phone booth, the class was roaring. And so was Ms. Waterman. She was laughing out loud. But I also saw something else in her eyes. Surprise. She hadn't been expecting this. Until then, I had just been another boy in her class. A fat boy, no less. But now I was this other thing: a boy who could hold the entire class in the palm of his hands and get them to do what he wanted them to do. And that, as she surely knew as our teacher, was no small feat.

But victories such as these are short-lived. After a few hours of warmth from Ms. Waterman and my classmates, I reverted back to being just another kid in a school of kids, some fat, some ugly, some slow, some weird, some as plain as the door we walked through each day, some possessed with beauty that was already, at nine years old, fading. There were no other plays to be written that year, no other creative outlets to show what I could do, and so I ate my cheeseburgers and eggs and bacon and fries and deep-fried pies, and I grew larger and larger and larger.

•

"Hey, fat ass!"

"Hey, Lardo!"

"Look at that boy! He's got tits!"

"You sure you're in the right place? This is the men's room, little girl."

Most of these insults came not from cruel children but from adults. They sat on their porches in the evening and yelled things out when I biked by. They yelled insults from their cars. They made comments when they saw me standing at a urinal.

I was in the fifth grade, and, admittedly, I had ballooned up. But I had also clearly passed some tipping point having to do with social acceptability because the insults were hurled every day, multiple times a day.

At one point my father suggested that I wear a bra.

"Bob!" my mother said in that tone that meant that he should stop talking right now.

"What?" my father said. "I'm not saying it to be mean. I'm just saying, aren't there bras for boys?"

I stomped out of the room, shutting and locking the bedroom door behind me. I could hear my parents arguing, their voices rising, until my father left the apartment, slamming the front door behind him.

Here's what I can tell you about being a fat boy. Other kids want to fight you, for no reason except that you're fat. It's also okay for people of all ages to laugh at you, in front of you, and to call you names. Even a dentist told my mother that I was disgusting and should be ashamed of myself. My mother, to her credit, took me to a new dentist. The more these episodes accumulated, the fatter I became. Fat begat fat.

Fifth grade, sixth grade, seventh grade—these were the fat years. The *really* fat years. I'd be lying if I didn't say that I was fascinated with it. My belly was huge, but it seemed like a thing unto itself, an alien life force that was clinging to the skinny me. Naked, I would take fistfuls of my fat into my hands and squeeze it. Or I would lift and drop a blob of belly. Or I would poke into my gut as far as I could. My belly button was like a sinkhole into which my entire finger might disappear. How had this come to be?

My weight had reached its critical mass the summer between seventh and eighth grade. I spent that summer in Memphis with my mother, who was taking care of my cousin while her father was in the hospital. I had heard stories of classmates who went away for the summer, met a cute girl, a girl cuter than any girl we knew at home, fell in love with said girl, and then did things with that girl that they hadn't been able to do with any of our girls at home, like using tongues to kiss. Or more. And so I had similar fantasies of finding such a girl in Memphis, a girl who might look like a slightly older Lisa Marie Presley, with a snarling lip and bedroom eyes like her father. My summer in Memphis would be a transformative time, a reinvention of my self-esteem, and I would return to Chicago with tales that would make me the envy of boys and a great mystery for girls to unlock. But none of my fantasies came to fruition. What, after all, had I been thinking? That girls in Memphis would like fat boys? That I would shed weight during the drive down to Memphis? That everyone in Memphis would be fat, making my weight an issue of relativeness?

I was in Memphis the summer after Elvis Presley died, and my aunt took me to Graceland, where she photographed me in front of Elvis's famous house. The photo pretty much sums up my sad state of affairs. I'm fatter than I've ever been; my orange T-shirt with the iron-on Elvis decal is bulging, turning a midweight Elvis into a misshapen Elvis; my prescription eyeglasses have tinted almost entirely black to shield the sun from my sensitive eyes; and my hair, which was longer than anyone in Memphis wore it back then, had curled into a Bozoish hairdo from the hours we had stood in line in the humidity. The photo was a Polaroid, so I saw instantly what a horror show I must have looked like to everyone. I looked absurd.

It wasn't until we returned to Chicago that I dared step on a scale. It was a scale where the numbers spun past you, slowing down once they hit your weight. When I saw 200 spin quickly by, I almost fell off the scale. Wait . . . what? I weighed over two hundred pounds? How was that even possible? I was eleven years old. Five feet four inches tall. A few months shy of twelve. And I weighed somewhere in the vicinity of 210 pounds. Holy frickin' crap!

The next day, I woke up early and started jogging. There was a trail behind our condos where the dangerous elements of our school hung out, but there was a slim-to-none chance that someone would wake up at five in the morning to jump a fat kid jogging. I took other measures to lose weight, too. I cut the amount of food I ate by half, and once I got used to eating half of what I normally ate, I cut it in half again. I even drank a raw egg one morning because Rocky Balboa had done that.

I started losing weight, but I still wasn't attracting girls. The lesson of fourth grade—writing and performing my play—wasn't lost on me, so I dove into projects to set myself apart from the other fat kids. The first project was to write a book. I began bringing to school writer guidelines that major publishers sent to me, letters from actors and directors who wrote to answer my questions about Abbott and Costello, and contracts from major studios who wanted to charge me exorbitant fees to reprint the still photographs from their movies. At first, my classmates didn't believe that I was actually, really and truly, writing a book, but after I continued bringing in these exhibits of my hard work, they couldn't deny that I was up to *something*.

The next thing I did to distinguish myself was try out for the school's annual talent show. As a boy whose voice quaked whenever he was called on, the very thought of getting up on stage in front of several hundred kids made me squirt pee into my Huskies. But it was something I knew I had to do. I had been a student of comedy my entire life (there's a photo of me in my crib wearing Groucho Marx glasses), from watching *Laugh-In* to memorizing George Carlin routines to buying Super 8 movies of Charlie Chaplin. I read books about comedians. Hell, I was *writing* a book about comedians. It was only natural then that I should try stand-up comedy at the talent show.

The first bit of business was to steal Steve Martin's best material and type it up. I didn't realize that stealing material was wrong. After all, I was a student of vaudeville, and it wasn't uncommon for comedians trained in vaudeville to use each other's material. And so in the grand tradition of vaudeville, I stole Steve Martin's stand-up act, cut it down to ten minutes, and modified it for a grade school audience.

All the while I exercised, continuing to lose weight. Even so, no one noticed. Or did they? One morning on the school's blacktop, a gaggle of girls stood off to the side, staring at me and whispering. Finally, one of the girls—a girl who had always been nice to me— walked over while her friends looked on. I expected her to say that she and her friends had noticed my weight loss. Perhaps they wondered what my secret was.

She glanced back at her friends before turning to face me. "The girls were wondering," she said. "Is your dick also fat?"

"You should see for yourself," I said. "And then you can report back to them."

My reply sent her running to her friends. I was pleased with my comeback. But something had made itself known to me that day, that I would always be fat to the kids who had known me as fat, and that I would have to complete my transformation before I started high school, at which point I could write off my grade school classmates as collateral damage in my life. By and large, they would no longer exist to me. I would shed the old me and leave behind the skin, along with nature's other evidence of decay, in the field I jogged each morning.

•

The talent show was a defining moment. A turning point. It was almost everything I had hoped for, except that I had taken second place and not first, losing to disco dancers. I had received a standing ovation. I did an encore. Even when I returned to my grade school twenty-three years later to talk to a gymnasium full of students about being a writer, the one thing every former teacher of mine remembered was the talent show, how until then they'd known me mostly as a kid too paralyzed by shyness to speak up in class, and how, on the day of the talent show, they had witnessed a nearly biblical transformation.

The talent show took place near the end of eighth grade. It was my grand finale. At the end of the school year, when I handed around my autograph book to get signed, many of the girls wrote how they couldn't wait to read my first book. "Don't forget me when you're famous," they wrote. A few wrote their numbers in the book so that I could call them over the summer.

I didn't call them. I worked on losing more weight. I focused my attention elsewhere, lusting for a high school girl I'd seen riding her bike around the park. I biked all over that summer, hoping to see this girl whose name I had learned through detective work. It was the summer of "My Sharona." It was the summer of "I Want You to Want Me." It was the summer of "The Logical Song," "Chuck E.'s in Love," and "Bad Girls." It was the summer that divided one life from the next, and when I began high school, I developed a new identity for myself, leaving the fat boy behind forever—or so I thought. But no matter how much weight I would lose or gain, no matter how many girlfriends or wives I would have, no matter how my social circles would change to include (on rare occasions) the celebrated, the wealthy, and the famous, the little fat boy would be always inside my head, standing off to the side of the room in his ill-fitting clothes, wondering what to say next or whether to speak at all. My shyness has been misinterpreted as stand-offishness; my self-consciousness as vanity. What I didn't realize then but do now is that I would always be that little fat boy. Every second of every day, he whispers in my ear. Every second of every day, there's no escaping him.

THE COWARD

I had this colleague at my last job: Vik. Professor of literature. Seventy years old. Short. A chain-smoker. A complete and utter asshole.

This last observation wasn't just my opinion; it was the opinion of many.

He was bitter, black hearted. People avoided him. He wasn't as smart as he liked to believe he was. Not even close. He'd published next to nothing. Not that I gave a shit, but he was quick to judge others, to place himself higher up some imaginary hierarchy, so there was that. For reasons I couldn't pinpoint, he decided he didn't like me. That was fine. I didn't like him, either. But his dislike took the form of stopping in front of my open office door to laugh derisively and shake his head before walking on to his office. I said nothing. I let it go. Was he crazy? I didn't know. But then he began knocking into me. On purpose. A body-check followed by a laugh. I said nothing at first because, well, surely this short, seventy-year-old man wasn't *really* body-checking me. Not on purpose. But no: The laugh that followed each body-check confirmed it. He meant it. The bastard *meant* it.

•

The first time I broke someone's nose was in a sanctioned fight—a Kenpo Kung Fu tournament. I was twelve. I had advanced to the final round, the round to determine first prize. After bowing to my opponent, I threw the first punch. The punch connected with his nose, and I felt it give way under my padded fist. The tournament was a noncontact event. The point of a noncontact tournament was to show control by punching close enough to the opponent to score points without actually making contact. Breaking my opponent's nose? It disqualified me. But since I had made it to the final round, I was still awarded the second-prize trophy. The kid with the bloodied, crooked nose would get the much larger trophy. It was the first time I realized that it was sometimes a better thing not to win.

Stand back in the shadows. Wait. Be patient, be patient, be patient.

•

Before joining Kenpo, I had studied karate with a sadistic man who had been an army drill sergeant. He had premature gray hair. He was in his late twenties or early thirties, and one day he walked across our backs while making us guess his age. When someone guessed too high, he jumped into the air and then landed on the unlucky guesser's back—a crushing blow to the spine. The recipient of the blow let out a howl or uttered "Oh God" and was slow getting up afterward. I knew how old he was, so I low-balled my guess. "Twenty?" I asked, and he laughed. "Smart kid," he said.

Because I was a big kid—by "big," I mean tall for my age and fat—the other younger kids, my sparring partners, weren't much of a challenge to me, so the sensei (the aforementioned sadistic fucker) threw me in to spar with the adults. The adults were ordered not to hold back on me.

My first sparring partner made the mistake of holding back.

I kicked him in the nuts and then moved in quickly for the kill, knocking him down and then raising my leg to stomp on his neck when the sensei, laughing, ordered me to stop.

"You see?" he said to the man on the ground. "He's not a kid. He's your opponent. Let down your guard and see what happens."

No one let down their guard against me again, no matter their size.

•

As I slid into my mother's car after school one day in the third grade, my mother's gaze remained fixed on a distant scene: the aftermath of a fight among grade school boys.

"I don't get it," she said.

I looked where she was looking. "What?"

She told me that she had seen two kids fighting. She had thought the other kids—the spectators—were going to jump in and help the weaker kid, but what they actually did horrified her. When the weaker kid began losing, the others jumped in to finish him off.

I nodded. What my mother said was true: I saw it all the time.

"That's terrible," my mother said.

I nodded again. It was. And because of this I knew I could never lose a fight. Losing wasn't an option.

•

I learned to fight dirty. In the seventh and eighth grade, there was a classmate who wanted to fight me every other week. He never won. One the one hand, I felt bad for him. Where I was tall and fat, he was short and fat. His clothes were shabby, and he smelled. He wasn't a bright kid, and he lived in a ramshackle house covered entirely in gray shingles, the only house of its kind in our neighborhood. On the other hand, his relentless desire to fight me was maddening.

We fought after school, and teachers sometimes wandered over to break it up, making us walk opposite ways home, even though we lived in the same direction. More often than not, however, the teachers didn't wander over, and the fight would continue. I didn't like punching people in the face, and I didn't ever want to get punched in the face, so I would run in quickly, put my opponent in a headlock, and then run forward until I hit his head on something hard—the corner post of a chain-link fence or a telephone pole. Usually, he yelled out for the fight to be over. If he didn't yell out, I would drop to my knees, and with his head still in a headlock, I'd rub his nose along a stretch of concrete, just enough to scrape it. Rubbing the opponent's nose across concrete was extremely effective psychological torture, inspiring panic, and it wouldn't take long before he was begging for the fight to be over.

But then, two weeks later, he'd inexplicably want to fight again. Why? I wondered. Why?

•

This asshole I worked with kept at it. Stopping at my office to peer in and laugh. Knocking into me in the hallway. Laughing derisively after doing so.

•

I can still feel my padded fist hitting my opponent's nose during the Kenpo tournament, his nose popping, blood flowing from his nostrils as his eyes filled with tears.

During my freshman year of high school, while I was walking back to a nighttime event at my high school, a car roared up in front of me, abruptly stopping, and five guys jumped out. Before I could assess what was happening, they ran toward me, knocked off my glasses, and started punching. It was more startling than painful, and it was over before I knew what had hit me. The attack was random and unprovoked, but even now, over thirty years later, I take stock of my surroundings whenever I'm out walking, and I pay acute attention to approaching cars.

Until recently, I had assumed my childhood was similar to everyone else's, and that most people, at one time or another, have been in fights—fights where knuckles hit bone—but I was wrong. In the world I presently move in—the rarified world of academia—most of my colleagues have never thrown a punch or been punched. Maybe this is why academia is a culture of passive-aggressive behavior, because so many of my fellow professors were never cornered in a gym locker room in high school for making a snide comment. They've never had their heads shoved in a toilet for turning something told to them in jest into political capital. There have never been consequences for behavior that's petty one day, manipulative the next.

•

While taking Kenpo, I learned to break boards. The instructors had organized public demonstrations that featured, among other things, me and another kid breaking boards for the benefit of a captive audience. We performed for Boy Scout troops, VFW members, grade schools.

There are two tricks for successfully breaking a board, the first of which involves how you pivot your wrist as your fist approaches the board. The final snap of the wrist makes a world of difference. The second trick is psychological. You have to imagine your hand not striking a board but rather going through the board, as though it were air, as though it were nothing. You have to imagine that there isn't even a board there.

Before I learned these two things, I was unable to break a board. I tried repeatedly, until my hand ballooned up and turned purple. Once I learned them, I was never not able to break a board. It was like slicing cake.

•

I should state here that I have never started a fight, never went out of my way to challenge someone to a fight, but I have always defended myself.

•

The asshole colleague knocks into me one day and laughs, and I follow him to the mailroom. I say loudly, "What in the fuck is your problem?"

He turns around and says, "You! You're my problem!" but I can tell he's scared. He doesn't actually look to see if he has any mail. Instead, he walks quickly back to his office. I match him step for step. I'm saying, "Why are you acting like you're in grade school? Huh?" I'm saying, "What the fuck's your problem, man?"

He says nothing until he steps inside his office—what he thinks is his safe zone—and then he turns around and says, "Go! Get!" flapping his hand as though shooing away a fly.

I don't move. I wait until he walks around his desk and sits down.

Once the old son of a bitch is settled, I point at him and say, "You do *not* want to fuck with me, man! I'm the last person you want to fuck with!"

When I turn to leave, I see heads of colleagues rapidly retreat into their offices. They were staring at someone they hadn't seen before—me—and they don't want me to catch them staring.

•

I still imagine the loser on his knees, the other kids rushing in to finish him off. *That won't be me*, I always thought.

•

I have no respect for chickenshits and cowards.

When I was in my early thirties, my then girlfriend bought a house in Iowa City, which sat next to a rental property. An indeterminate number of college students lived there. They were mostly eighth-year juniors: a herd of unambitious and utterly self-centered dudes who, several times a week, kept us awake all night long. I tried being cool at first; I tried talking to them. I said, "Hey, look, you want to party? Fine. But maybe we can figure out some schedule? Maybe if you give us a heads-up we can stay out late ourselves?" But at three, four in the morning, I'd look outside and find them sitting on my front porch or leaning against my car, or they'd be standing in front of our house drunkenly yelling about one stupid thing or another. I remember overhearing an argument one early morning: "I'll break you in two! I'll break you in two!" This was repeated over and over and over, but apparently no one ever came to blows.

In the years that we lived there, my anger toward them escalated. They were tough when they were in a large group, but they were always silent when alone. One of the loudest—and probably the dumbest, although such a distinction was difficult to make—was a scrawny kid who puffed up like a blowfish whenever he was with his roomies. He would direct smart-ass comments at me, barely loud enough for me to hear, until I was at my door and walking inside, and then he'd get a bit more vocal.

A week before my girlfriend and I moved out of the house, I was walking home and saw the scrawny fucker sitting alone on the patio. He was holding a guitar. He and his roommates were always holding guitars, plucking away and looking around, as though a film crew were nearby capturing it all. Their front porch was raised, so I walked up to where he sat but remained at street level, and I said, "You think you're a tough guy when your buddies are around, don't you? If you've got something to say to me, you come over to my house and knock on the door, but come alone. I'll be waiting for you."

I started walking to my house. As soon as my foot touched the first step, Scrawny yelled through his screen door, "Hey, guys, I think we got a problem here. Someone wants to fight!"

By the time I reached my door, four more of my neighbors had joined Scrawny on the porch. They began yelling: "What's the problem? You want to fight? Is that it?"

I wasn't dumb; I wasn't going to invite five guys to come over and fight me.

Chickenshit, I thought, shaking my head. Typical fucking chickenshit.

•

My last fight—my last *real* fight—didn't go well.

I was in college. This would have been 1986. I was twenty.

There was a bowling alley in Carbondale, Illinois, that offered a weekly special: all you could drink and bowl for six dollars. Six dollars!

Week after week, I went. And week after week, I made sure to get my six dollars' worth.

Back at the apartment complex after a night bowling and drinking, I encountered two guys looking for trouble. The apartment complex was notorious for its parties, and on any given night it was likely you'd encounter dudes looking for trouble.

I'm not a violent drunk. I am, in fact, the guy whose mood usually improves with each drink. But not that night. I have no memory of what the guys said to me, but I didn't like it. I have some memory—a dim one—of being taunted. And I clearly remember saying (foolishly), "C'mon, motherfuckers!"

You hear people say they didn't know what hit them. Well, I didn't know what hit me.

I was facedown on the ground. I thought my jaw was shattered. The dudes were gone by the time I stood up. When I touched my jaw, my hand became instantly wet, but from what? I had landed on dry concrete. There wasn't a drop of water anywhere.

And then I saw it: blood streaming from my chin. Blood cascading.

I rushed to my apartment and looked at myself in the mirror. A large chunk of skin on my chin was missing. There was no flap of flesh, no cut. Just . . . nothing.

At the emergency room, the doctor said, "Have you been drinking?"

"A little," I said, smiling. The doctor didn't smile. He was disgusted with me. He took a sheet that covered my entire face, except for my chin, and dropped it on me. And then he and a nurse went to work: scrubbing grit out of the wound with what felt like a steel pad; dabbing the blood; injecting needles into the open wound; sewing me up.

Twenty-seven stitches, when all was said and done.

•

When I was in grade school, a high school kid killed one of his classmates with a baseball bat while other classmates stood by and watched it happen. I don't remember who the murderer was, but the kid who was killed was one of my brother's classmates.

No episode from my childhood held more power, and I suspect it's why I always anticipate the worst. In any given situation, I tend to wonder, "What's the worst thing that can happen right now? How badly can this go?" To not be prepared for the worst might mean being approached by someone with a baseball bat and surrounded by onlookers who most likely won't help you.

•

The gears of academia don't grind slowly. They simply never grind at all.

I wrote a detailed complaint to my immediate boss about Vik's behavior. Nothing happened. I wrote a similar complaint to the next person higher up, the dean. Again, nothing. It took securing a job offer from another university and then threatening to leave before the university's second in command took action, but the action taken was to bump the problem back down to my immediate boss, who reluctantly met with Vik. In that meeting, Vik admitted to laughing at me but denied repeatedly knocking into me. He claimed that he would refrain from this behavior in the future, which he agreed was childish.

Did he refrain?

No.

A few years later, I had to file yet another complaint, this time cc'ing the e-mail to him so that he could see what I had written while forcing the administration's hand to do something. When I approached Vik in the interim to see if he was done with his bullshit, he stared up at me in a poor attempt at acting and said, "Why, I think you're making all of this up, John. I don't know what you're talking about."

•

Like every other bully I have ever met, he was a coward. A sad little coward.

•

The fist hitting the nose. The nose giving way, snapping. The blood pouring from the nose.

For weeks, months, I couldn't stop thinking about the karate tournament and putting myself in my opponent's place, his world briefly dissolving to darkness as blood poured from his nose, followed by a painful throb.

•

Every year the scar on my chin grows more pronounced.

•

I spent most of my twenties hanging out in bars and have seen my share of bar fights. Over time, I became good at guessing who would win. Once, in Iowa City, at a bar called Gabe's, my friend and I sat on opposite sides of a booth, watching two strangers play pool. We watched for hours, but early on, within the first thirty minutes, I sensed they would eventually fight. One guy looked pretty normal—flannel shirt, jeans, work boots. He was a solid-looking guy, tall, probably a construction worker. The other guy was bat-shit crazy. You could see it in his eyes. Like Rasputin's. Like Manson's. He kept taunting the other guy, testing him, pushing it, trying to get a rise out of him. I'd never seen him before, which increased the odds that a fight would go down.

I said to my friend, "Want to bet?"

"On the game?"

"No. On the fight. It's going to happen."

"Okay," my friend said.

"Twenty bucks," I said.

My friend laughed, nodded. "Who do you want?"

"I want the crazy dude."

"Okay. I'll take the other guy."

We sat there for several more hours. Sure enough, Crazy got a rise out of Normal, and toward the exit they headed. My friend and I downed the last of our beer, stood, put on our coats, and started walking toward the front door, but Crazy was already walking back inside, laughing, euphoric.

"My guy must have run away," my friend said.

"No," I said, "I don't think so."

We opened the front door, and there was my friend's pick. He was on the ground, facedown, knocked out cold. A trickle of blood dripped from his mouth. The fight must have lasted two seconds. Three tops.

Standing over the body, my friend pulled out his wallet, removed a twenty-dollar bill, and handed it to me.

•

Freshman year of high school, I was friends with a tough little fucker. Max. He was a good kid from a bad home, and he wouldn't punch someone unless compelled to do so. In math class, a kid behind him had begun to pick on him, so Max weaved a hard plastic Bic pen around his fingers, forcing his middle finger further down than the others, and then he turned around and smashed the pen as hard as he could against the kid's nose, breaking the pen in two.

I liked being friends with Max. And for reasons I no longer remember, Max liked being friends with me.

In art class later that year, a kid named Will tried picking a fight with Max. It was one of those uninitiated fights that happens in grade school and high school, where one person gets an idea to fight and won't let it go, like an itch he can't reach or a voice inside his head saying Fight him, fight him, fight him. Will was quite a bit taller than Max. He had blond hair parted to the side and wore plastic-framed glasses. Max smiled and said, "Nah, you don't want to fight me." But Will wouldn't let it go. The itch was there; you could see it in his eyes, the madness at being unable to reach it. Will said, "After class. Me and you." Max laughed. I laughed too, nervously.

After class, Will walked out first and then spun quickly around, waiting for Max to leave the classroom.

Max, stepping into the hallway, said, "I'll give you one last chance to keep walking."

Will looked around at his friends, smiling, puffing himself up. "Nuh-uh," he said.

"Okay," Max said. Before Will could put up his fists, Max connected with a right-handed roundhouse punch. Will's glasses broke in two, and like some cheap comic prop, the two pieces flew in opposite directions. Will's nose had clearly broken, too, and his head slammed into a locker before he fell hard to the ground.

"You done?" Max asked. "You want more?"

Will, trying to hold back tears, shook his head. No, no, no.

Max and I walked away, stepping over Will's lanky legs.

What I admired about my friend Max was his reluctance to go into a fight, his fearlessness once he did go into a fight, and then his restraint. One punch. He'd made his point, so why move in for the kill? But also: Why risk losing a fight you'd already won?

Reluctance, fearlessness, and restraint. A code to live by.

•

Stand back in the shadows.

•

The difficulty of living in this world is that it's full of chickenshits and cowards. The difficulty is that you can't always punch someone who deserves to be punched. The difficulty is that, at some point, you have to concede failure and move on, even when that failure gnaws at you. As adults, we can no longer play by the golden blacktop rule: If someone pushes you, you have the right to knock him on his ass. On the black-top, there's no eye for an eye; it's two eyes and a kneecap for an eye. A soul for an eye.

I'm not an advocate of violence in any form, but I can't help thinking that some people would be better citizens if someone, at some point, had given them a good beating, as my friend Max did to Will for his mindless taunting. Did Will ever challenge another boy to a fight? Not that I saw. In fact, he kept his big mouth shut for the rest of high school. And you know what? He was a better kid for it.

•

Wait.

•

The George W. Bush years were winding down. It was a new school year, and when I saw Professor Vik for the first time that semester without any of our colleagues around, he started grinning, as he did whenever he saw me, grinning that stupid shit-eating grin, as though my very presence entertained him. Of course, I knew what he was doing. He was trying to get under my skin. And in the past he had. Because he's a coward. Because he knew I wouldn't risk my job and punch him. Because the administration had proven itself to be spine-less fuckwads for not punishing him. Rumor had it that Vik had done this before to other colleagues, colleagues who had retired or were now dead—the laughing, the knocking into—yet there he still was, enjoying his tenure, unscathed except for a ridiculous slap on the wrist. But when I saw him this time, I saw a man already pummeled—not at the hands of an enemy but by the pathetic and sad smallness of his own life. What, after all, did this man have? His career was winding down, and he had nothing to show for it, nothing to distinguish himself as anything more than mediocre. All he had was the contempt of his colleagues. Even those few he considered friends, like the professor he gossiped with each morning, talked shit about him behind his back. For a chain smoker, he had outlived the prediction of his insurance company's actuary life expectancy table, but for how much longer? Another two years? Five? And who among us would go to his funeral? One of my long-suffering colleagues told me she checked the newspaper every day for his obituary. Would this be Vik's legacy? That the people with whom he worked couldn't wait for him to die? What a wasted life. This fact, it seemed to me, was far more devastating than any physical blow could ever be.

•

Be patient, be patient, be patient.

•

I'm not proud of the fights I've been in, but it would be a lie to say they haven't shaped the person I am today. I have no intention of ever throwing another punch, but I am always prepared to do so should someone else throw one. And I still look around at everyday objects to see what kinds of weapons they could become in a pinch. You never know when you'll need that thick book to be a rock to the back of someone's head; that bottle, a club to the face; that pen, a knife through the heart.

PART THREE
The Fat Boy's Education

LIKE A MAN

In the fall of 1971, my father made a grave mistake. He decided that our family should move from Chicago to Houston.

Stories about Houston's wonders floated north from my aunt and uncle who had moved there a year earlier: the construction boom, the remarkable weather, the money that could be made. My father was a roofer, and not only would he be able to earn a better hourly wage, he would likely be able to work year-round, something that was impossible in Chicago once the brutal cold and snow moved in, often as early as November and lingering as late as April some years. For my father, moving to Houston must have felt like what moving to Deadwood, South Dakota, was to prospectors who'd heard tales of gold in the Black Hills. We'd be crazy not to move there!

I was one month into first grade when we moved. For reasons I no longer remember, my father and brother lit out for Houston weeks before my mother and I did. My mother drove the two of us in our 1964 Rambler American. I loved that car and had made my mother promise that she'd give it to me when I got my driver's license in twelve years. She agreed. My mother was pragmatic that way. She knew that the car likely wouldn't last twelve more years, and she knew I likely wouldn't want the car by then, so why not just tell me that I could have it?

Our first stop was in Memphis, where we spent the night with relatives, and then we continued on to Houston, driving well into the dark, the illuminated green exit signs streaming past like a scene in a movie. My mother, a lifelong smoker and speeder, smoked Winstons and sped the entire way. She was thirty-six years old and skeptical of my father's decision, as she was of most of my father's decisions. But the move to Houston was a grand adventure for me, albeit one that I didn't fully grasp. My mother woke me in the early morning, before the sun had started to rise, and led me to my aunt and uncle's front door—a house where wealthy people might have lived, surrounded by palm trees and lush foliage like nothing I had ever seen in Chicago. In fact, there were no trees of any kind anywhere near the apartment we had moved from, and the greatest expanse of grass was on the slope that led up to where the Stevenson Expressway met Harlem Avenue. I was five years old, and for the first time the move to Houston made sense. We were going to live like rich people!

•

Of course, we weren't going to live like rich people, but my parents did upgrade by moving us into our very first house. The house looked nothing like my aunt and uncle's—ours was small and ugly—but it was significantly larger than the apartment we'd moved out of, larger than the mobile home that had burned down, larger than the rented basement my parents were living in when I was born, and for the first time in my almost six years on the planet, I had my own bedroom.

Back in Chicago, I would venture outside on my own all the time, but in Houston I was confined to our driveway and yard. Our first week there I played in the driveway until I saw a tarantula parked on the asphalt. When the tarantula saw me, it began walking slowly toward me with its huge, fuzzy legs. I screamed and ran inside. And there I stayed, wearing my Houston Oilers pajamas and playing with my only remaining toys, among them a rosy-cheeked Dapper Dan doll whose clothes and plastic shoes you could take off and put back on. I was probably too old for a Dapper Dan doll, whose purpose was to teach me basic life skills, but so be it. I wasn't so much interested in what a toy could teach me as I was in giving it a backstory, like how Dapper Dan had moved from Chicago and was afraid of tarantulas, and how he wished he lived in Dressy Bessy's house, which was so much nicer than his own. My leisurely days of playing with Dapper Dan and giving him a life of his own came abruptly to an end, however, when my mother took me to my new school.

My new school was experimental insofar that the classrooms, with a few exceptions, didn't have walls. These rooms were separated by partitions, which meant that if you were tall enough, you could stand up and see all of the classrooms at once. The exceptions included music and gym classes, which had their own self-contained rooms.

At my previous school, I would stay in the same classroom all day long, but in the new school, I would have to walk to a different classroom for each subject, except that there was no door for walking into a room. In lieu of a printed schedule, I was told to follow a girl named Heather.

"She's in all the same classes as you," Ms. Guidry, my homeroom teacher, told me on the first day, "so you just follow her to your next class." Ms. Guidry was a little older than my kindergarten teacher, Ms. Gonzales, but not by much. They even looked alike, with their dark hair piled high on their heads. But Ms. Guidry scared me. Where Ms. Gonzales would have put her hand on my head and crouched down to talk to me, Ms. Guidry's eyes were burning with something that I couldn't yet articulate, and her voice made it clear that I was there to obey or suffer the consequences.

I nodded. Heather, who was missing a few baby teeth, smiled.

Once it came time for me to follow Heather, however, Heather and her friends turned around and told me to get lost. Back in Chicago, I was friends with all the girls in my class, but down in Houston, I apparently talked funny and dressed funny, and my hair was too long. After being told to get lost, I hung back from them. At first, I was able to follow the girls from a distance, but whenever they fell out of sight, which was most of the time, I would stand outside the music room and walk in with a large group, trying but failing to hide from the teacher. Some days I would walk in and out of that same room multiple times, attending music class right after I had just attended music class. The teacher looked exasperated each time I showed back up, but he didn't say anything, so I would take a seat in the back row and pay close attention.

To make my class day more confusing, I would sometimes be snatched up by the school's psychiatrist, who put me through a battery of tests. Most of the tests involved wearing headphones and listening to a tape recording and pressing buttons. I never understood what the tests were for, and I always felt sick to my stomach while taking them because I could never find the answer I was looking for. And then, without any further directions, I would be told to run along to my next class, despite having no idea what my next class was or where it would be.

And so the day would go: I'd get ditched by the girls, I'd go to music class, I'd take tests I didn't understand. I felt on the brink of crying most of the time, but I didn't. I held it in.

One day on the bus, I sat on the side with the girls. When the bus driver looked up into his huge rearview mirror and saw what I'd done, he told me to get on the other side.

"With the boys!" he yelled. "You *are* a boy, aren't you?"

Everyone laughed.

When I stood, the bus driver hit the brakes, and I fell to the ground, landing on my chin. Again, everyone laughed.

After school, I begged my mother to let me stay home the next day.

"I can't do that," she said. But my mother hated Houston, too. She claimed it was her health, that the humidity was causing her problems, and while I believe that this was true, I also believe that she hated Houston itself. She had grown up in and around Memphis and, after moving north, had vowed never to return to the South again. Whenever someone in Chicago complimented her accent, my mother would reply, "What accent?" She rarely admitted that she was from the South. She tried, as best as she could, to assimilate up north, to blend in, and part of the North's appeal was that no one was in her business. She could be invisible. But now here she was, back in the South, and as much as anyone might tell her that Houston was different, she knew better.

One day after school, I started drawing all over my bedroom wall with a crayon. I knew that what I was doing was wrong, but I couldn't stop. I drew up and down, large squiggles and shapes. When my mother saw what I had done, she said, "Johnny, this isn't like you. You know better than this."

I nodded. I did know better.

My mother cleaned the crayon from the wall before my father saw it, and I quit drawing on my walls, but I spent more and more time in my room. I withdrew. I spent less time in my own head and more time inside Dapper Dan's, but Dapper Dan wasn't happy, either. In fact, he hated school, too, and would often sit around naked next to his pile of ridiculous clothes, unable to do much of anything except stare at the bedroom wall he so much wanted to scribble on. It was all Dapper Dan could do not to pick up a damn crayon and cover every inch of that blank, offensive wall.

•

For two more weeks, I went dutifully to school—always lost, always confused. One day after music class, the teacher said, "You can't come back in here. You need to find the class you're supposed to be in."

He didn't offer to help, and I didn't ask. And so I walked to one of the partitioned rooms where gloomy students my own age sat. With nowhere else to go, I walked inside and took a seat. The teacher, who was young and pretty but looked angry, said, "This isn't your class." When I didn't say anything, she sighed heavily and began her lecture.

Once class was over, I returned to the music room, but the teacher simply shook his head, so I followed some boys I recognized toward the gym. By now, I had begun crying. I had never before, until that point, cried in school. I barely remembered ever crying, except when I was two years old. I was a stoic little boy who normally sucked it up, but I couldn't do it anymore. I broke down. While standing in a long line that snaked into the gymnasium, I cried more than I had ever cried before. A gym teacher, wearing a whistle, a tight polo shirt, and navy shorts walked up to me, leaned down, and said, "Quit crying. Act like a man."

I quit crying. Or tried to.

The line moved slowly. I had never gone to this school's gym class and wasn't sure why we had to stand in line to enter the room. Once I stepped inside the gymnasium, I saw neither basketballs nor jump ropes but rather a stool, a backdrop, and a photographer with a huge camera set up on a tripod, ready to take my official first grade photo.

In my photo, the entire front of my shirt is wet from crying. My eyes are red and puffy. I'm trying to smile, but it's obvious that I'm really trying not to cry. In fact, I'm ever-so-slightly biting my bottom lip while my upper lip looks as though it might have been quivering. I look like the saddest boy who had ever stepped foot in Houston.

At the end of what had been a mind-numbingly horrible day, I heard someone calling my name, but I ignored it. I kept walking. Students I didn't even know told me that Ms. Guidry, my homeroom teacher, was calling for me, but I didn't stop. Heather said, "You better go see what she wants or you'll be in a lot of trouble."

I finally stopped. I turned around. By now, Ms. Guidry had caught up with me. She grabbed my face and squeezed it hard, until my lips became fishlike.

"You don't ignore me, boy," she said. And then she began shaking my head back and forth. "Why haven't you been going to the same classes as Heather? Huh? Why did you ignore what I told you to do? Why do you think you can do whatever you want?" She let go of my face by shoving my head, causing me to stumble backward.

I didn't cry, though. I didn't cry because I knew that I would never go back to that school. I would never let Ms. Guidry grab my face and squeeze it ever again. Something cold descended into my chest, and there it remained.

On my way out, some of the boys offered words of sympathy, but once I stepped onto the bus, I found Heather, who grinned at the sight of me, eating up every last bit of my misery.

•

Clearly, I represented to Ms. Guidry something more than what I was. I was a northerner, a little boy without a southern twang and with long hair by Houston's standards of the day, a boy whose clothes were evidence of parents who weren't flush with oil money. Did she think my parents were hippies? Did she think we were freeloaders who had finagled our way into a school that was above my pedigree?

The next day when my mother dropped me off at the corner for the bus, I waited until she left, and then I walked away. I did this for two days. I have no memory of where I went or what I did. I was a five-year-old boy somewhere in Houston, spending my day looking for something to do until the bus arrived, at which point I could return to the corner and wait for my mother, who would come outside once she saw or heard the bus drive past our house.

Eventually, someone from school called my home, and the ruse was up. I had to explain to my mother what had happened.

"I'm not going back," I yelled. "I'm not going back! I'm not going back!"

When my father came home from work, my mother told him what had happened and said, "He's not going back, Bob. I won't let him."

I don't know what else my mother said to my father, but I didn't go back, and by the end of the month, we returned north to Burbank, and I enrolled in first grade at my third school in less than four months. The principal wanted to hold me back, but my mother insisted that I would be fine.

And I was fine, although I never viewed adults the same after Texas. That was over forty years ago. I don't have to act like a man now; I am a man. I'm almost fifty-two years old, six feet tall, and two hundred and fifty pounds, but in the fall of 1971, after returning to Illinois, I was only five years old, a few days shy of turning six. I was a boy. My new classrooms had walls and a door and several windows. And a cursive alphabet chart above the chalkboard. And girls who liked me did my homework for me to help keep me from failing; girls who saw the fear in my eyes and wanted to save me. And save me they did.

ON BEING A LAZY FUCK

My grade school's annual science fair presented me with a reality that I didn't want to face—namely, that I had neither the interest nor the brain power to construct something as elaborate as a smoking volcano or a potato-powered clock. I wasn't a dumb kid, but I was lazy. I was so lazy, I often borrowed my best friend's homework so that I could copy it, not because I didn't know how to do it but rather because the idea of doing it exhausted me. One time, my friend lost the homework that I had copied from him, so he borrowed mine, which was really his, so that he could copy it before it was to be turned in. When I saw our teacher walking down the aisle to see what we were up to, I turned away, and when the teacher saw Joe copying my homework and said, "Joe! What are you doing?" I turned toward Joe, feigned outrage, snatched back my homework, and said, "Joe! What are you doing?" So not only was I lazy, I was the worst imaginable friend, someone who would sell you down the river for a laugh.

But until seventh grade, my laziness had not registered on any of my teachers' radars. The only person who had caught wind of it was my mother. Whenever I had a big project due, such as a portfolio on the country of Colombia, I would wait until the very last moment and then, having waited, stay awake all night.

My mother, who had begun picking cotton at the age of three, left home at thirteen to take a full-time job, and spent her work years on a factory assembly line, would look at me in horror in these instances, as though she had given birth to an actual sloth.

"Why do you do this to yourself, Johnny?" she would ask. "How long have you known about this?"

"I know," I would say each time. "I know, I know, I know."

"But why?"

"I *know*," I would say, getting irritated, the already limited time before me ticking away.

"Okay then," my mother would say. "But you realize that you age yourself about ten years each time you do this."

"Thanks," I'd say.

And then my mother would wag her head and leave me alone.

But she was right. I did age. My breathing became labored as I ran out of time. The lack of sleep made my thinking muddy. I would eat an entire box of Ding Dongs and drink a dozen Diet Pepsis while I worked, only to feel intense gastronomical pain by morning. Why indeed had I done this to myself?

But none of my previous demonstrations of laziness compared to what was to come in the seventh grade. The science fair, which featured only seventh and eighth graders, was one of the highlights of the year, a time to wander the gymnasium after lunchbreak to witness the ingenuity of our own, and some of my classmates spent weeks, if not months, preparing their projects. They enlisted the help of their parents, who sometimes showed up to school during lunchtime to assemble whatever insane display they had concocted. Wasn't that cheating? I wondered. Nonetheless, there were years you might have thought the Manhattan Project was on display in the gymnasium of Jacqueline Bouvier Kennedy Grade School, and that a mushroom cloud, produced by dozens of smoke bombs, might appear on the blacktop during recess, suggesting radioactivity. Who knew what my classmates were capable of?

I did not spend months on my project. I did not spend weeks. I did not spend a day or even an hour. I waited so long that the amount of time that I could dedicate to my project was the time I had remaining for my lunch hour—in short, an hour minus the time my mother spent picking me up and then dropping me off.

Instead of sacrificing time, I sacrificed food, which, likely, would have been a can of Spaghetti Oh's. I loved Spaghetti Oh's. I would eat all of the pasta and orange sauce, leaving the spongy but delicious meat-balls for last, and then I would eat three of those at a time, hoping that the sum total of meatballs would be divisible by three, but, alas, it rarely was. But I did not eat Spaghetti Oh's the day of the science fair, nor did I eat Chef Boy-r-Dee's Beef Raviolis, another favorite, or a delicious grilled cheese sandwich. I ate nothing. And I resented it.

"Why do you do this to yourself, Johnny?" my mother asked. "How long have you known about this?"

"I know," I said. "I know, I know, I know."

"But why?"

"I *know*," I said, irritated.

I had decided that morning, while sitting in my reading class, that my project would be about the Loch Ness monster. Did it cross my mind that the Loch Ness monster had nothing to do with science? No, it did not. It was an animal, wasn't it? And wasn't an animal, whether real or imagined, some subset of science? Why, of course it was. Wasn't it?

And so I took some leftover clay from an art project, and I shaped it into what looked like the Loch Ness monster if the Loch Ness monster had no distinctive details whatsoever, which is to say what the Loch Ness monster would look like if it were an earthworm. Next, I typed out two paragraphs about the Loch Ness monster, which I had taken directly from a book titled *The Mystery of the Loch Ness Monster* by Jeanne Benedick. I placed the one-page tome in a clear plastic cover to give my presentation the air of professionalism. And then I asked my mother to give me a ride back to school.

My mother looked over my three items—the indistinct clay worm, the plagiarized history, and the unread copy of *The Mystery of the Loch Ness Monster*—and then she looked up at me and shook her head. Whatever hope she'd held out for me, whatever dreams she'd been banking on, all of them swirled down the drain.

"I'm going to be late," I told her.

"I don't understand you, Johnny," she said.

"Me neither," I said.

At school, inside the gymnasium, I set up my three items on one of the lunch tables. On either side of me, my classmates set up their beakers, bottles of hydrogen peroxide and vinegar, boxes of baking soda, and other assorted essential science fair items. When I looked down at my clay worm, I felt the depth of my laziness, but I decided not to let my own acknowledgment of failure show in my demeanor, so I sat up straight and waited for the masses to file into the gym.

As expected, most of the younger kids gathered around the smoking volcano. A few kids paused to look at my clay sculpture, only to ask, "What is it?"

I would point to the title of the book and say, "It's the Loch Ness monster."

And then they would move along. I might as well have said, "It's Millard Fillmore." Or, "It's a whale penis."

One by one, the teachers who knew me stopped, examined my project, then looked up at me, as dismayed as my mother, before walking away without a word. My gym teacher and science teacher, both of whom had been athletes and enjoyed heckling kids, stopped at my display. They looked at each other, then back down at the display.

"What the hell is this?" the gym teacher asked me.

The science teacher said, "McNally, McNally, McNally. What's going to become of you?"

And then the two of them laughed and moved on.

Shortly before the fair was to end, a young teacher stopped at my table and closely examined all that I had to offer. I didn't know her, which led me to believe she taught first or second grade, maybe third or fourth—grades I had toiled away at at other schools. I could tell she took pity on me, and that her stopping was an act of kindness.

"This is very interesting," she said, reading the purloined description. Then she looked at my clay sculpture as though she were in a museum, squinting and nodding. I said nothing. When she finally looked up at me, a fat boy with curly red hair and prescription glasses that darkened in the sunlight, she said, "So tell me. Do you think the Loch Ness monster really exists? Or do you think it's a hoax?"

I could have confessed that I didn't know jack squat about the Loch Ness monster, that I had slapped the entire project together in about thirty minutes, which should have been as obvious to her as it clearly was to everyone else who had stopped to look at it. Or I could have transcended my own laziness and relished her with long, detailed histories of Loch Ness monster sightings, describing the Scottish landscape with such description she might have thought that I had transported her to a marshy bank as a thick, ominous fog rolled over her. But I did neither. I shrugged and grunted. I made a noise that sort of sounded like "I don't know." And then I pushed the book toward her, the only person that day who had shown me any kindness, and said, "You want to know more? Read this."

As soon the words left my mouth, I realized that I had screwed up.

"I mean," I began, fumbling for what I might possibly have meant, but it was too late.

The young teacher said, "No thanks," pursed her lips, and walked away.

Well, I thought and, calling it a day, gathered up my stuff. I took the clay tube and tossed it in the trash along with the sheet I had typed up, but I kept the book with me, carrying it to my next class so that I could have something to flip through.

That book—the very copy I took to the science fair that day—is next to me as I type this. On its cover is a very old drawing of the monster attacking a ship. The red words *Loch Ness Monster* look three-dimensional against the green background. The book is water damaged, as though it had been submerged in the Great Glen itself, home to the supposed beast. I have owned the book for almost forty years now. I've moved it to ten states, packing it and unpacking it each time. Published in 1976 by Xerox Education Publications, it is only 128 pages long. The contents are mostly drawings, charts, and photos. The font is large.

I still haven't read it.

SWEET BIONIC JESUS

For a while, everyone was concerned about my soul.

By the time I turned six in 1971, I'd not yet been baptized. My mother had grown up Baptist but didn't like how, according to her, nosy and judgmental the Baptists were. My father had grown up Catholic but had dropped out of high school because of how cruelly the nuns had treated him. With the exception of *Rosemary's Baby*, which I had seen at the Sheridan Drive-In when I was three years old, I'd had no memory of religion or God or Jesus or the devil prior to first grade, but once I turned six years old and still had not been baptized, several people (an aunt, a friend of the family, my mother's coworkers) brought up the issue of my soul. It was as though they were all part of the same coven, not unlike the men and women committed to Rosemary's pregnancy, and all of their attention made me feel special.

Before long, I was standing in line at Saint Fabian Church in Bridgeview, the only non-baby among the soon to be saved, waiting my turn with godparents I barely knew: a friend of my mother, a Mexican woman who worked alongside her at the factory, making corrugated boxes, and her husband, who was from Mexico City and spoke very little English. The priest who baptized me was an old man with tiny spectacles behind which his small, wet eyes blinked like a kitten's. I had started the morning of my baptism as a six-year-old condemned to hell, but after the priest touched my head with holy water, I was pretty much guaranteed a spot in that loveliest of lovely places—heaven. My soul, at long last, had been saved. Amen! Amen!

•

What I had thought would be a minor disruption to my childhood, a disruption I welcomed because cake and presents were involved, turned into the protracted and laborious process of becoming a full-fledged Catholic. Next on my plate would be weekly CCD classes, year after year, leading me toward reconciliation and then, later, if I had the necessary faith and stamina, confirmation. But here's my first confession: I enjoyed it. At first.

During those first few years, the classes took place on Sunday mornings, which were no big deal since nothing terribly interesting was ever on TV. In fact, the only show I remember ever watching on Sunday was *The Magic Flute*. The best I could tell, *The Magic Flute* was about a boy from outer space who had magical powers and spoke a made-up language. It wasn't until I was an adult that I realized that the show was for Jewish kids and the language was Yiddish. How was I to know? I wouldn't meet anyone Jewish until I went away to college. In fact, other than one Muslim friend, everyone I knew in my Chicago suburb was Catholic. Because of this, I had assumed that most people in the world were Catholic. I was, it turned out, wrong.

But those first few years—during second and third grades—were glorious! Oh, how I loved church. I loved shaking strangers' hands during the midmass meet and greet. I loved saying, "Peace be with you." I loved shopping for the little books of illustrated Bible parables out in the lobby. I loved the holy water. I loved the aspergillum, that weird club-like device that the priest shakes holy water out of when he's walking up and down the aisles. I loved it all, but my absolute favorite was guitar mass.

Guitar mass brought out the shaggy-haired high school kids and their twelve-string guitars and bongos. I expected one of them to bring a double-neck electric, like the kind Jimmy Page played during "Stairway to Heaven," but, sadly, this never happened. They would sing songs from *Godspell*, like "Day by Day," and the parishioners, many of whom were cute high school girls, would sing along loudly. The priest for guitar mass wasn't the ancient Father O'Meara who had baptized me but rather a young priest with a bushy mustache, long frizzy hair, and a receding hairline. He looked like Meathead from *All in the Family*, a resemblance that comforted me because I liked Meathead. Unlike Rob Reiner's Meathead, our hippy-looking priest wasn't angry, and he didn't yell at us. In fact, he was soft-spoken and nervous.

Meanwhile, in CCD, we watched a movie about a dying girl and, if I'm remembering correctly, a moth that turned into a butterfly. The point of the movie wasn't lost on me, even at that young age, and the first three times I saw it, I was moved by the death of the girl and the arrival of the butterfly. Or whatever happened.

What I most looked forward to was the day that I could participate in the eating of the wafer. But in order to do this, I would have to go to confession. Really? The very thought of it made me want to poop my pants. I would have to go into a dark booth and tell the priest all the horrible things I'd done? Really? *Really?* Despite my gastrointestinal hesitance, I still wanted that damn wafer.

In preparation for the day that I could participate in communion, I tried making my own wafers out of Wonder Bread. From a slice of fresh bread, I would cut out several circles and then pound them with the side of my fist until they were, well, not quite hard liked a wafer but definitely flat like one. And then I would eat them. One Sunday after church, I ate half a loaf of Wonder Bread, stopping only to vomit. I realized, of course, that the priest would be handing me only one wafer, not a bag of wafers, and that the purpose of eating the wafer wasn't to throw up. And yet throw up I did, as though purging my body of its demons.

Around this same time, I had watched on TV for the first time *Soylent Green*, the futuristic dystopian movie about overpopulation and the rationing of a food source known as Soylent Green. At the end of the movie, we come to realize that the tasty green wafer is made out of human corpses. Throughout childhood, I filtered nearly everything I learned through the lens of pop culture, and so when I learned that the wafer at church was made out of the body of Christ, it was only natural for me to connect this bizarre and fantastical detail with the Charleton Heston movie, but I told this to no one. I must have known that yelling out "Soylent Green is people!" in church would have set me back in reaching my own goal, which was to stand before the priest as he said, "The body of Christ," to which I would reply, simply and humbly and not in horror, "Amen."

•

The first serious fracture in my until-then-unwavering faith was the story of the prodigal son. The way I saw it, the good son—the son who had stayed at home and busted his ass—doesn't get rewarded for his loyalty and hard work while the scumbag brother who screws up at every turn gets a party thrown for him when he comes rolling back to town. What was up with that shit?

I remember feeling outraged at the very idea. What kind of moral was this? I even offered up my cynical conclusion: "So, I should be like the bad kid?"

"Well, no," my mother said, to which I mordantly replied, "Nope. That's what God wants."

In short, I called bullshit on the story of the prodigal son, which opened up a door that I couldn't close. Suddenly, everything was up for debate.

Around this time, my mother had developed life-threatening health problems. Blood clots in her leg needed to be stopped before they worked their way up to her heart. I was warned, before her surgery, that she might not survive. I was in second grade. For obvious reasons, my mother's religious resolve strengthened. For reasons less obvious, my brother and I began living with my Aunt Peggy and Uncle Lloyd in the nearby suburb of Justice while my mother was hospitalized.

One Sunday, my aunt took me to *her* church. She was Baptist and didn't believe that my Catholic baptism was valid and wanted me to be baptized—*legitimately* baptized—in the Baptist church, but her church scared the holy hell out of me. Instead of talking in a soft, muted voice and telling nice stories, the preacher paced back and forth, yelling, holding the Bible above his head in such a way I expected him to use it as a weapon and crack somebody's skull with it. Furthermore, the baptism involved what appeared to be a swimming pool into which I would have to be dunked entirely backward, submerged under water for a good while, and then brought back up, gasping and heaving, into the light. I made it clear to my aunt that I wasn't getting near that man or his pool of sadism. Where my mother viewed me as a sentient creature capable of making intelligent decisions, Peggy saw me as a bratty, defiant child who was used to getting coddled.

When my mother came home from the hospital, she doubled-down on the Catholic Church. She took all the necessary steps toward conversion. My mother, who had always struggled with her weight, had dropped dozens of pounds while in the hospital, and when I now look at photos from that post-hospital period—photos in which she is standing alongside the church's sisters, who wore trendy but tasteful clothes instead of the penguin-like garb of old—my mother looks almost unrecognizable. She also looks happy.

But the happier and thinner my mother became, the less happy and fatter I became. It was as though together we needed to maintain the exact same weight and level of happiness, and if one of us dipped, the other one surged.

•

The things that I liked about the church either failed to keep my interest now, had changed, or were gone. The priest who looked like Meathead had moved to another parish; we had begun going to regular services instead of guitar mass; I owned all of the illustrated Bible story books and now preferred celebrity stories about actors who played the Fonz and Ralph Malph; and the people whose hands I once enjoyed shaking had become loathsome creatures who gossiped in the church parking lot after mass. Worst of all was that my CCD classes were now on a weeknight instead of the weekend, and this struck me as a cruel punishment, having to attend yet another class after having spent all day in school. My boredom during these classes was excruciating. OhMyGodOhMyGodOhMyGodOhMyGod, I would think. OhMyGodOhMyGodOhMyGodOhMyGod.

Despite this, I successfully made it through my first confession, even though, short on juicy admissions of guilt, I lied about the things I had done. Even while on my knees in the confessional and speaking to the priest through the semidarkened scrim, I knew that lying during my first confession was probably the worst thing I could have done, but so be it. I was told to say five Hail Marys, but since I never got around to memorizing the Hail Mary, I kneeled at one of the pews and waited until enough time had presumably passed for me to have said the prayer five times, and then I guiltily returned to my parents.

Because I had successfully completed my confession, I could, at long last, stand in line and accept communion ("The body of Christ. The blood of Christ"), and I was still excited to take the wafer on my tongue ("Soylent Green is people!"), but after that first time, it lost its appeal. I was changing into a different person, but what kind of person? I wasn't sure.

I wasn't the only one who noticed this metamorphosis, either. My teachers at my regular school noticed. Instead of being the shy, quiet boy who dutifully did his homework and only occasionally squirted pee in his pants, I had turned into a loud, wild-eyed fat boy who laughed at everything and who, annoyed by the boy sitting in front of him, cracked him across the head with his own ruler, which was made of thick plastic. It was fourth grade, and I quit caring. Or, rather, I cared only about those things I considered worthy of my attention. All the rest? Here, let me fart in their general direction.

I carried this bad attitude over into CCD—especially CCD—where the moral lessons bored me beyond belief. I began making fun of the movie about the dying girl and the caterpillar or moth or whatever it was. When the caterpillar or moth or whatever appeared after her death, I would say to anyone close to me, "Look. She's back!" Each year, my jokes during the movie grew louder until the Sister who taught the class took me by the arm and marched me into the main office.

"Would you like me to tell Father O'Meara about this?"

I shrugged.

"Is that a yes?"

"No," I said. "I guess not."

But the truth was, I really didn't care. Tell him? Don't tell him? It didn't make a difference to me. Getting kicked out of CCD wasn't like getting kicked out of my real school. I *wanted* to get kicked out of CCD. I was bored with Jesus. Bored with God. I was already having my doubts about them both. I had quit paying attention so long ago that by this time I wasn't even sure I remembered what their relationship was to each other. Was Jesus the son? But why did some people say Jesus is Lord? Wasn't God the Lord? The only reason I even knew the word *lord* with any intimacy was because my parents would sometimes talk about someone "lording it over" someone else, and because my Aunt Peggy would say, nearly every time I saw her, "Lordy, Lordy, Lordy, Lordy." And then there was Tarzan, Lord of the Jungle.

In the fifth grade, I began saying *goddamn it* with some frequency. If I dropped a book on the playground, I would say, "Goddamn it!" and then look around, hoping someone had heard me. If someone said something to me that I didn't like, I would say under breath, "Goddamn Mike" or "Goddamn Mary" right after he or she had walked away. "Texas Love Song" by Elton John had "goddamn it" in the lyrics, so I began playing it repeatedly and singing it loudly. What I wanted was a sign that God would strike me down, a lightning bolt across the blacktop, the tip of it touching my head and killing me in front of all the girls I had crushes on. "Goddamn it," I would say when lightning didn't strike me. "Goddamn it, goddamn it, goddamn it."

I also began to have other obligations. I had enrolled in karate classes. After a year of these classes, I began doing karate demonstrations for other kids, which involved performing a choreographed routine, flipping someone, and breaking a board in two. Next to the condominium on Seventy-Seventh Street was a woodworking shop, and I would stop in once a week to ask for spare boards so that I could spend my spare time breaking them. In other words, I was busy. I had better things to do.

I'm not sure what, if anything, the church could have done to have renewed the vigor that had possessed me at six and seven years old, but the final blow for the church as an institution was when Saint Fabian scheduled CCD during *The Bionic Woman*. If ever I needed an excuse to give up on church altogether, this was it.

I'd like to tell you that I'm being flippant, but I'm not. The fact is, my faith wasn't there. I didn't feel it. And I didn't care about *not* feeling it. All I needed was an external excuse to say, "Look, I've warned you about wasting my time, but you didn't take me seriously, and now you've really gone and done it by pitting yourself against the one TV show I was most looking forward to!" And it *was* the one TV show I was most looking forward to, too. This was long before Hulu or TiVo, and exorbitantly expensive video cassette recorders had barely entered the marketplace. In short, if I missed an episode of *The Bionic Woman*, it was possible I might never see the show again, unless the station ran reruns, which didn't always happen back then. And so I clung to my anger.

While I could express my annoyance to my peers, I couldn't admit the truth. I was surrounded by kids who didn't question their faith or the existence of God. Had I ever had faith? Had I ever believed? I had liked the novelty of it, but now that the novelty of it had worn off, I felt like the walking dead each time I stepped into church. I went through the motions while trying to stay awake.

At home, I begged my mother to let me quit going to CCD and church, but she wouldn't relent.

"Once you go through confirmation," she said, "I'll leave it up to you whether to go or not."

Confirmation was one of seven sacraments. The others included Baptism, the Eucharist, Penance, Anointing of the Sick, Holy Orders, and Matrimony. I'd already checked two off the list.

"Really?" I said, skeptical. Should I have asked for these terms in writing?

"I won't be happy if you quit going," my mother said, "but I'll leave the decision up to you."

"Okay," I said, smiling.

"Don't be so happy about it," she said.

"What?" I said, trying not to look happy.

"I know you," she said.

But did she? By giving me a choice, she must have held out some tiny nugget of hope that something might happen in the meantime to change my mind. Did my mother think I would have an epiphany? That I would see God's hand—his actual hand—reach down from a cloud and point at me? Because if I had seen that—if I'd seen his actual hand—I'd have kept going to church. Short of that, I would sever all ties and work on getting my life back—what was left of it.

What this pact with my mother achieved, however, was a stepping up on my part. No more fooling around. No more horseplay during CCD. No more pining for Lindsay Wagner. No more making fun of the movie about the dead girl and the bug or whatever. No, I wanted to get through this confirmation without a hitch. I even scaled back how many times a day I said "goddamn it."

When time came to choose a confirmation name, I chose "John Paul." I chose it because it was the only name of a pope that I knew, and because there had been two John Pauls in a row: John Paul I, who died after only a month as pope, and John Paul II. My name, therefore, would be John John Paul Raymond McNally.

"Why don't you pick a name that doesn't have 'John' in it already?" my mother asked.

I shrugged. "Nah. I like it."

And so I remained John John Paul.

•

I'll be honest. I have no memory of confirmation. I have no memory of what it entailed, what the ceremony was like, or what its point was. This speaks not to my age but to how little I cared. True, I had thrown myself into it, but I had done so in order never to go to church again.

What I do remember is the party afterward.

It's dark out. My 35-millimeter camera hangs from a strap around my neck. Our relatives and friends fill our tiny condo. There's cake for me. And presents. My dog, Shoo Shoo, has hidden under my parents' bed. Not long after the party has started, after everyone, except for me, is smoking and talking loudly, I notice an odd flickering light. I open the sliding glass door that leads to our patio. The woodworking business—the place I would go for boards to break—is on fire. The only thing separating the woodworking business from the condos was the narrow road that led to the parking spaces.

I climb over our patio's wrought-iron fence and walk closer to the fire. This is when I hear sirens. The fire truck's streaming lights fill the air. I lift my camera and take a few photos, but then I realize that a fire of this magnitude and proximity on the night of my confirmation is a sign. It's not exactly an actual hand reaching down from a cloud, but it's a sign nonetheless, and although I'm not sure from whom the sign is, I decide to interpret it as a sign that I should never go to church again. This is it, I think. This is my sign. I'm in the clear.

Back at the condo, I head for my parent's bedroom and kneel down at the side of the bed, as though to pray, but then I lower myself to my side, lift the bedspread, and meet my dog's eyes.

"Shoo Shoo," I say. "Want a treat?"

Shoo Shoo's tail wags.

"Okay," I say. "But you have to come out and get it."

Shoo Shoo's tail stops wagging. I already know she won't come out for the treat. It's too much effort. I reach under the bed and hand the treat to her. I hoist myself up and head back to the party.

"Here he is!" I hear someone say. "Johnny! Come, look!"

Like Rosemary approaching the coven to view her baby for the first time, I move toward them hesitantly, but as the small gathering of relatives and friends part, I see that it's only a cake with a frosted cross awaiting a sharp knife and the mouths of multitudes. Slice by slice, I divide the cake among them all.

PART FOUR
The Fat Boy's Sex Life

THE KINDERGARTEN OF
EARTHLY DELIGHTS

I don't tell love stories. But here's one.

In 1970, when I was five years old, I fell in love with all the girls in my kindergarten class. I loved the ones who looked like they could have been on magazine covers. I loved the tomboys, the brainy ones, the wild ones. I especially loved the wild ones. The wild ones wore dresses with loud colors and crazy patterns and their hair was untamable. There was a feral look in their eyes that said, Let's climb that jungle gym, stand on top of it, and scream as loud as we can!

Most of all, I was in love with my kindergarten teacher, Ms. Mendoza. She was young, probably in her early twenties. She had dark eyebrows and wore her dark hair in a beehive. Her makeup sparkled. In my only photo of her, she's wearing a tight pink polyester dress with a high collar, sexy and prim at the same time, like a British woman from one of the Hammer Horror movies that I watched on Sunday afternoons, a woman who might have been a member of high society at the movie's beginning but by the movie's end would be a bloodsucking vampire showing a good amount of cleavage. When I was five years old, I loved cleavage, and I loved vampires, and I loved prim women who turned into vampires after other vampires had bitten their necks. I wanted to bite Ms. Mendoza's neck. I wanted to suck her blood. I wanted to sink my fangs into her and fill up like a tick and then rest my head against the cleavage she never showed us. Was this so wrong?

•

We lived in Summit, Illinois—a foul-smelling southwest Chicago suburb that was home to the Argo Baking Powder and Corn Starch factory. The whole area reeked from the noxious vapors that rose like genies from its smokestacks.

Summit is probably most famous as the setting for Ernest Hemingway's story "The Killers." The story is about, among other things, mobsters, for whom, historically, Summit became a hiding place during Prohibition. The grade school where I attended kindergarten was just down the street from the factory, and a little farther down that same street were several lunchrooms and taverns, like the ones in Hemingway's story.

Our family had recently moved into an apartment under an expressway. I don't remember having any friends in the neighborhood that year. Mostly, I spent time alone, which was fine. I liked—and still like—spending time alone. It was during these stretches, with nothing planned and no one to play with, that my imagination thrived and the seeds of storytelling were planted.

Railroad tracks ran behind our apartment, a few feet beyond the parking lot, and I would stand close to the rails and yell for chalk each time a train rolled by. Back then, freight train cars would be marked up with chalk to inform the switchmen where the cars needed to go, and if a conductor had any spare chalk with him, he'd throw it out the window for me, usually a hunk half as big as my small head, and I would then write all over sidewalks and Dumpsters with it. Other times, I would climb the steep incline to Harlem Avenue, the major road that intersected the expressway that took you downtown, and I would raise my first over my head and gesture for passing semi drivers to honk their horns. This was how I entertained myself when I was five years old. If I wasn't doing one or the other, I might be strategically placing a penny on the railroad track and then waiting for a train to run over it, or I would be patrolling the neighborhood with a can of Silly String. I loved my can of Silly String, but I used it sparingly because my mother told me that it would be the only can she would ever buy me. "It's too expensive," she said, "so enjoy it while it lasts." When an older boy came up and demanded that I give it to him, I raised the can and sprayed him in the face, as though he were a bug. The boy, whose face was covered with green strings of foam, screamed in fright and took off running.

One afternoon, I sat on the kitchen floor playing while my mother talked on the phone to my Aunt Peggy. My mother was leaning against the counter and smoking a cigarette. While she smoked and talked, I played with a train that I had made in kindergarten using construction paper and brass fasteners that held the different train cars together. If I placed it flat on the floor, the train would curve when I moved it quickly. The train, I imagined, ran along the tracks behind our apartment. I had invented two characters for whom I used two different voices. One character was the train conductor. The other character was a man who simply asked questions.

The man who asked questions said, "What you got in that train?"

The conductor said, "Oh, just some drugs."

The man who asked questions said, "Where are you taking those drugs?"

The conductor said, "Oh, just gonna take them to the drug pusher."

I heard my mother say to my aunt, "Hold on a second, Peggy." When I looked up at my mother, she was staring at me as though I were not her son but rather an imposter, a boy who looked remarkably like her son but who was, upon closer examination, not her son at all.

My mother said, "What're you doing, Johnny?"

"Playing," I said.

"What're you playing?" she asked.

I smiled. "Drug pusher," I said, having given my story a name. It was the first time I could remember having come up with a wholly original story that had a setting and a cast of characters.

My mother, keeping her eyes on me, said into the phone, "I got to go, Peggy. I'll call you later." After hanging up the receiver, my mother approached me cautiously, suspiciously. "How do you know about drugs?" she asked.

"Wait here," I said.

I ran to the bedroom that I shared with my older brother, collected the evidence, and ran back to the kitchen, happy to accommodate. What I handed her were pamphlets that warned against drug use, but the warnings were not what had caught my attention. What appealed to me were photos of colorful pills and mountains of powder. I also loved the wavy images that made everything look like a funhouse mirror. Best of all were the hippie girls. One of them on the pamphlet looked sad, sitting in a corner and putting a needle in her arm, and I wanted to pet her head and say something comforting like "Now, now." Another girl looked like she was having a lot of fun trying to fly out her apartment window, and I wished I was jumping out the window with her. I knew from the TV news what drugs were and what drug pushers did, but the pamphlets were full of such spellbinding photos that I didn't care what the words actually said, only that drugs looked like fun. A lot of fun.

"You know that drugs are bad," my mother said.

I smiled and nodded.

"Why don't you have the train carry something else then?" she suggested.

"Okay," I said.

My mother dialed my aunt again. I looked up at her and said, "Choo! Choo!" but when my mother finally turned her back to me I said under my breath, "Where's the drug pusher?" and then I answered myself: "Around the corner, sir."

•

The same year that I spun propaganda-inspired tales of freight trains and drug mules was also the year that I created a simple but effective sexual fantasy to which I would put myself to sleep each night. In that fantasy, I'm the only boy in a nudist colony. I am five years old. The other nudists include the girls in my kindergarten class. Ms. Mendoza is also nude and sitting on a large boulder while the girls in my class sit naked around her.

When the girls see me, they smile and call out: "John! John! Come here! Join us!" I obey. I stroll over. I, too, am naked, and the first person I greet is Ms. Mendoza. She pats her thigh, and I climb up onto her lap. It doesn't occur to me that sitting naked on a large, jagged boulder might be uncomfortable for her, or that adding the weight of a child to her lap would be unbearable. This is a fantasy, a story, so there is no pain at the nudist colony, only pleasure. I sit on her lap and make myself comfortable.

Ms. Mendoza strokes my hair and says, "You're so cute. You're the cutest boy in the whole class." And then she does something quite amazing. She lifts me up over her head, as though I'm a beach ball, and passes me around to the naked girls, who giggle as they reach for me, and I giggle when they touch me, their fingers gently pressing into me, tickling me. I look down and see them all—Lisa and Veronica and Marcy and Kimberly—all the girls I love, and all of them naked! I am as weightless as air. The girls love passing me around. It's erotic, it's sexual, although these words are not in my vocabulary. I sense that it's different. I sense that this is new terrain. And I want them to keeping passing me back and forth. I want them to pass me around forever.

•

I had crushes on all of the girls in kindergarten except for one. She and her brother were both in my class, but neither spoke a word. Not a single word. In their school photos, they look Eastern European and are dressed in tattered clothes—the boy in a vest you'd imagine Oliver Twist wearing, the girl in a sweater that could have been handed down several generations. They look like really tiny old people. They have the saddest expressions I've ever seen, and in their individual photos, they are each frowning the way refugee children frown in wartime photos. There were a lot of immigrants where I lived, and the possibility was great that they didn't speak English, that they didn't have any idea what anyone was saying. There was, to my knowledge, no ESL class back then. They had likely been taken away from their friends back in Poland or wherever and dropped into this strange room with wooden pedal cars, an oversized copy of *Dick and Jane* resting on an easel, and an ever-smiling woman with a beehive hairdo; and, likely, none of it made any sense. I worried about them. I worried about them a lot, in fact, often telling my mother about them. I worried, but I did not have a crush on the girl. Having a crush on her would have been like having a crush on somebody's grandmother. It would have been wrong. But the rest of the girls? I wanted to remain naked with them at my own private nudist colony, like the ones I'd seen on the nightly news. It was on TV where I learned about these nudist colonies. They were in California and Florida, but there were not any in Illinois, certainly not in Chicago along the shores of Lake Michigan. I wanted to spend my life as the sole boy in a nudist colony full of girls and women, not just with Ms. Mendoza and my classmates but also Ginger and Mary Ann from *Gilligan's Island*, the girls from *The Partridge Family* (including Mrs. Partridge, for whom I also lusted), *The Brady Bunch* girls, and the Flying Nun. Especially the Flying Nun. I wanted all of them to remove their clothes and habits, to strip down in front of me, a five-year-old boy with bright red hair and an ambiguous gleam in his lazy left eye. I would have been forty-four inches tall and forty-four pounds. A pound for every inch. I am monochromatic in my kindergarten photo, wearing a harvest gold shirt with a harvest gold clip-on tie. My mother had attached a darker tie to my shirt that morning, but when we arrived at school and I opened the car door, the tie fell off and landed in a puddle. My mother rushed me home and put a tie on me that blended in with the shirt, which is why I looked vaguely futuristic in 1970.

My mother was a kind and loving but unsentimental woman. My very first childhood memory was of the day she returned to work. I was two. She had taken a job working second shift at the corrugated box factory, and when she left me with my father, I screamed for hours. I screamed as though I were being lowered into a pot of boiling water. I didn't fear or dislike my father, but I had spent every moment of my first two years with my mother, and my father was not my mother. Exhausted from screaming and crying, I finally fell asleep on the couch. I remember being so tired that everything became dreamy through my smeared vision. And then I don't remember anything else for another year.

My attachment to my mother, however, remained steadfast. The year I was in kindergarten, I made her promise that she would wait outside for me. I attended the morning session, and each morning my mother dropped me off.

"Promise," I would say.

"Yes, Johnny," my mother would reply, not hiding any of her exasperation. "Of course I'll wait here."

Years later, my mother confessed that she had not waited for me. Ever. Not even once. I was in high school when she told me this, and I was deeply hurt.

"I had too much to do," she told me. "Sometimes I'd put laundry in the trunk before you woke up in the morning. Other times I went shopping."

Even though I knew by then that asking her to wait for me was unreasonable, I still felt betrayed.

"You never waited?" I asked. "Not even once?"

My mother shook her head. Nope.

"A couple of times," she said, "I'd be running late and worried I wouldn't get back there before they let you out. Or I'd get caught in traffic. And then I'd rack my brain trying to think up a story to tell you." She took a long drag off her cigarette and smiled at her own deviousness. "I always made it back, though," she said. "It never came to that."

I wonder what sort of little boy I would have been had I known my mother wasn't waiting nearby. Would I have been as afraid and sad as the brother and sister who never spoke a word? Would I not have fallen in love with Ms. Mendoza or the other girls in my class, too worried that my mother might have left me behind for good, that she wasn't ever coming back?

•

I was hospitalized three times the year I was in kindergarten. Once for pneumonia, once for dehydration, and once for a tonsillectomy. I remember, after the tonsillectomy, waking up in a room near a man who looked dead. He was probably still asleep from his own surgery, deeply anesthetized, but the way the white blanket covered him, the way his eyes were shut, and the way he didn't appear to be breathing all confirmed for me that he had stopped breathing long ago. I had spent that year staying up late on Saturday nights to watch Creature Features on WGN, and each Saturday at ten-thirty I would watch, until I fell asleep, an old black-and-white horror movie. My parents would put me to bed much earlier, but I would stay up, sneak out to the living room after they had gone into their bedroom, and then click on our tiny black-and-white TV. I always fell asleep on the couch, and one or the other of my parents must have carried me back to the bed I shared with my brother, but we never spoke of this. Thanks to the movies on Creature Features, I had seen my fair share of dead people as well as living dead people. After watching those movies, I'd begun to convince myself that everyday objects were monsters—a coat dangling on a hook in a dark room was the Wolf Man waiting for me to shut my eyes before he pounced; a shadow coming from my open closet was the Creature from the Black Lagoon who just so happened to be hanging out in there. If the man next to me in the hospital room wasn't dead, then surely he was a vampire. I opened my mouth to scream, but the pain in my throat was too great, and I shut my mouth. Shortly thereafter, I fell back asleep.

Each time I returned to my kindergarten class after a hospital stay, I would be even more popular with the girls, more popular with Ms. Mendoza. It was as though I were surrounded by a magical glow that everyone wanted to bathe in. Oh, how they loved me!

One day, the sad little boy who never talked mumbled, "Excuse me," on his way to the bathroom, and I yelled out, "He spoke! He spoke!" I had recently watched the old *Frankenstein* movie with Boris Karloff, and I would walk around our apartment yelling, "It's alive! It's alive!" and so I yelled "He spoke! He spoke!" in the same dramatic way that Dr. Frankenstein had yelled after he'd brought the monster to life.

Ms. Mendoza said, "Hush, John. Don't make a big deal out of it."

But it was a big deal. Or it should have been. The boy had never spoken before, and I was the first one to hear him speak. More than anything, though, my feelings were now hurt. This woman I loved—this woman I fell asleep to each night imagining naked—had just told me to hush. To make matters worse, she trivialized what I had thought was important. I wanted to cry, but I didn't. I must have looked like I wanted to cry, however, because Ms. Mendoza eventually wandered over to me, crouched down, and said, "It's better not to make a big deal of it, is all. That way, he'll feel comfortable talking." I nodded. I wanted to hug her; I wanted her to hug me. "Okay," I said, holding back tears. "Okay." It would be the exact same thing I would say to my first real girlfriend eleven years later when she told me that she thought we should just be friends. *Okay* would forever after be the word I'd most associate with heartache, this single word repeated twice, four syllables that would crush me in an instant because it meant that something that had once been wonderful had now come to an end.

•

I'm tempted to say that my recurring nighttime fantasy was my first explicitly sexual fantasy, but, except for the nudity, it wasn't explicit at all. The explicitness was in what it suggested and the effect of what it suggested had on me. This was the power of the story I had told myself. Each night, I would refine it. I might add a dog, like the one in the Coppertone billboard that featured a cartoon girl getting her bikini bottoms pulled down by the feisty, enviable mutt. Or I might let the girls keep their jewelry on but nothing else. I would tweak it, just a little, and then I would play out the scenario, falling asleep only after they had lifted me over their heads.

After kindergarten, I attended first grade at the same school for only a month. My best friend was one of the wild girls from kindergarten, a girl named Veronica, but then my life sped up, resembling, if it were a montage in a movie, the wavy, funhouse mirror of those drug pamphlets: a few months in Houston, Texas, and then back to a different southwest suburb of Chicago, where the principal considered holding me back a year because I was so far behind. My mother insisted that I would catch up, and catch up I did, with the help of a girl named Kristina Rochette, who had a crush on all the boys and would do their homework for them. And though I had a crush on Kristina, I still pined for Ms. Mendoza and the girls of kindergarten. I studied every detail of them from their class photos: the mole on Denise's cheek, the pearls Brigette wore, the way wild Veronica's bangs were parted. I even studied the sad brother and sister, their ill-fitting clothes, these two old people who had been shrunk down to the size of children.

A year passed. I begged my mother to take me to open house at the school where I had attended kindergarten. Open house was not normally for students who no longer attended the school, but my mother would occasionally indulge me, sometimes at my own peril, as though to teach me about the nature of consequences for doing improper things. And so we went.

In the hallway I saw Veronica, wild girl of my heart. I smiled and yelled her name and then I ran over to her.

A little over a year had passed since I had last seen her, and she did not remember me. She had that look in her eyes that said *save me* as she sidled up next to her mother. She was wearing a similar dress to the one she had worn in her kindergarten photo, a multicolored affair, and though she still parted her bangs in the middle, she looked ever-so-slightly different, the way identical twins look different after you get to know them. But the simple truth is that she looked different only because she had gotten older.

It wouldn't be the last time that my memory of someone would be stronger than their memory of me. This is the fate of a child who frequently changes schools. Kids from my previous schools loomed large in my imagination like supporting characters in a play in which I was the star, but I was often nothing more to them than a stagehand, easily forgotten. I didn't yet understand any of this the day that I returned to my old school. I just figured something horrible had happened to Veronica since we'd last seen each other, and that she had mistaken me for the person who had done the horrible thing to her. I wanted to reach out, touch her, and reassure her that it was only me, her old friend, but I refrained for fear that she would flinch.

Spooked by Veronica's reaction, I told my mother that I didn't want to see Ms. Mendoza anymore, but my mother wouldn't have any of it.

"Now, Johnny. We didn't come all the way out here just to turn around and go home," she said. "Let's go see her."

We walked into her classroom. She was finishing up with a boy I didn't know, talking to the boys' parents, as I stood there shivering. When it was my turn, I walked up to her, stuck out my hand to shake hers, and said, "Do you remember me?"

"Of course I remember you," she said. "John! It's so nice to see you. What a pleasant surprise." She crouched down to my height and said, "You were so good in my class. I wish I had an entire classroom full of little boys as nice as you."

I saw for the very first time love in her eyes, and I imagined us getting married and growing old together. I would introduce her to my friends. "This is my wife—Ms. Mendoza," I would say. "She was my kindergarten teacher. Imagine that!"

She patted my head now and stood back up. To my mother, she said, "Such a good boy. Thank you so much for coming by."

"He really wanted to see you," my mother said.

I shook Ms. Mendoza's hand good-bye, and when I pumped it, she smiled and laughed. It wasn't a mean laugh. It was conspiratorial, as though she knew that I was in possession of a great big secret about the two of us and she had finally figured out what that secret was.

She loves me, I thought. Everything will be fine.

This was the story that I told myself, at least. This was the story I most wanted to believe. Never mind that my mother had probably phoned ahead to warn Ms. Mendoza of our arrival. Never mind that I would never see Ms. Mendoza or any of the girls from my kindergarten class ever again. Never mind that my life is now full of such people to whom I have said, "Okay. Okay." The stories we tell ourselves are powerful drugs, and this one was my opiate, my addiction. I wanted to believe that it was a love story and not, as it surely was and is, a story about heartache, embarrassment, failure, and humiliation, none of which I knew about back then. I only knew about love and not love, and I knew which one made me feel good. I knew which one I wanted.

Later that night, and on many subsequent nights, I returned to that colony of beautiful girls. They had been waiting for the arrival of the only boy they had ever loved, a boy who, by merely showing up, would brighten their already sunny day.

"John," they would call out to me. "Come here!"

Sitting in the brightest patch of sunlight would be Ms. Mendoza, smiling, waiting.

"Join us, John!" the girls would say. "Hurry!"

And like the good little boy that I tried so hard to be, I obeyed each and every naked one of them.

ON THE RECORD

My mother enjoyed telling the story of my early love of music, how when I was a baby, Bobby Darin's hit song "Splish Splash" would turn a very unhappy baby Johnny into a happy, gurgling baby Johnny. When my mother accidentally broke the record, however, I became an inconsolable monster. I cried, I howled, I threw things. Since the record was several years old, my mother had to scour used record stores all over Chicago until, at long last, she found a copy, and, upon hearing it, I once more became a happy, gurgling baby.

My own memories of music love include asking Santa Claus for a Janis Joplin album; seeing Tiny Tim in person at a department store promoting his 1968 album *God Bless, Tiny Tim*; saving up money to buy my own 45s at Kmart; and holding a huge tape recorder close to my tiny transistor radio so that I could record my favorite songs. But nothing beat going to an actual record store, where rows and rows of bins were stuffed full of hundreds of albums, possibly thousands, and I wanted all of them.

The first record store that I shopped at with any regularity was located in the basement of Ford City Shopping Center. The basement was called Peacock Alley—a zig-zaggy trail of counterculture stores that wound under the mall's parking lot: a perfect refuge for teenagers and hippies. I always knew I was getting close to the record store—an open air shop surrounded by a short, wrought-iron barrier—because I could smell incense, which burned at the checkout counter, producing a thin trail of smoke. They sold pipes, too. And rolling paper. And posters of W. C. Fields wearing a tall Abe Lincoln hat and peeking up from playing cards gripped in his gloved hands. And fuzzy posters of the Led Zeppelin logo. And strobe lights. The women who shopped there wore fringe and loose-fitting burlap blouses and jeans whose cuffs were as large as their waists. They smelled like beer-scented shampoo and strawberries and marijuana. I was five or six or seven years old, and I lusted after all of them. I wanted to press my head against their soft bellies and sleep on their laps. My ultimate fantasy was for all of us to live together in the basement of that mall, just me and a few dozen hippie girls. We could eat every day at Nickelodeon Pizza and drink huge fountain sodas and sleep in the mattress store. Together, we would be one big happy family.

What could be better?

•

I lusted after women, but I was obsessed with albums. Occasionally, these two things—what I lusted for and what I was obsessed with—merged together. I was eight years old, for instance, when I saw Roxy Music's album *Country Life* for the first time, featuring on its cover two seminaked women.

The woman on the left is wearing a white bra and white underwear. Though her left hand covers her crotch, you can still see the dark outline of pubic hair. Her right arm rests against her forehead, palm facing out, as though she's overheated. Furthermore, you can see her nipples through the sheer fabric of her bra. The woman on the right isn't wearing a bra at all, only sheer black underwear, and she covers her breasts with her palms. Her nails are painted red. For some reason I can't grasp, the two women are standing in front of a fern. Even though I wasn't sure why, I found the fern an exotic and titillating addition nonetheless.

At eight years old I didn't understand the concept of horniness nor did I understand the logistics of sex, but my body responded accordingly. I probably didn't even make a conscious connection between what I was looking at and whatever was going on in my pants. It's like seeing a plane explode in the sky and gasping. One event merely follows the other. I would study every inch of that album cover until I thought I noticed someone watching me, and then I would quickly thrust it back into the bin and walk awkwardly away.

Also in the bins was David Bowie's album *Pin Ups*. Although there were no naked women on the cover, I knew better than to hold this album out in plain view, either, and so I would surreptitiously examine the image of the shirtless couple, Bowie and Twiggy, both of them wearing make-up that outlined their faces so that they appeared as two parts of the same person: where Bowie's face was darker from the makeup, Twiggy's was lighter; and where the rest of Twiggy's head and body were darker from makeup, Bowie's was pale. In the photo, Twiggy is leaning her head on Bowie's shoulder. She looks almost bored. Bowie, on the other hand, has an intensity in his eyes that you can't ignore. I didn't know at the time about the injury to his eye that had caused one of his pupils to be larger than the other. All I knew was that I couldn't stop staring into his eyes. It was as though he were hypnotizing me from the album cover. His red, shoulder-length hair is spiky on top, but most startling is that he doesn't have any eyebrows. What kind of person doesn't have eyebrows? Since I didn't know who David Bowie was (his name on the album's cover was, simply, "Bowie"), I wasn't even sure if he was a man or a woman. And precisely because of that ambiguity, I couldn't stop looking at him. It was my first encounter with androgyny, and I was fascinated by it, mostly because I wasn't sure how I was supposed to feel. Was I attracted to David Bowie or was I repelled by him? I didn't know. I felt a little of both. To be caught staring at this album would be worse, in some way, than staring at the naked women on the Roxy Music album, even though I wasn't sure why. Sexual ambiguity wasn't something that had crossed my mind. As with *Country Life*, I was furtive in my actions, sometimes holding another album on top of it so that I could easily cover the Bowie album should someone walk up behind me. Horniness turned me into a clever and sneaky little boy.

Perhaps the most taboo album covers were by the Ohio Players, an all-black funk-soul group whose cover art almost always featured a naked or nearly naked black woman. These felt especially forbidden because I was a fat little white boy who grew up in a neighborhood of fat little white boys, and yet of all the albums in the store the Ohio Players's called loudest to me.

On the cover of their album *Pleasure* is a naked woman with her arms above her head, head thrown back, eyes closed. Her head is entirely shaved. But when you open the cover, you realize that the woman's wrists are bound together with a heavy chain while the chain hangs from something we can't see. The cover for the album *Climax* features the same model in what appears to be a sexual embrace with a man kissing her neck, but when you open the cover, you see that she has stabbed the man in his back with a phallic-shaped dagger. I would stare at these covers and then flip them over to see the wrists chained together or the dagger thrust into the man's back, and, as with the Bowie album cover whose purpose was unclear to me, I felt equally confused and compelled. I was drawn to those images that made me feel one way and then, when viewed in a larger context, another way—especially when those things were at odds with each other. What drew me to these covers weren't just the commingling of sex and danger but also the story that was implied. Why was this woman chained up? Why was she stabbing this man? And how did all of these covers, which featured the same model, add up to tell a story? Something more was going on here than was meeting the eye, but I couldn't quite put my finger on it. The titles of those early albums—*Pain, Climax, Ecstasy, Pleasure*—were clues, too. But eventually I would move on to an area of the store that was less suspicious, like the display of posters, where no one would suspect I was up to no good.

•

These days, I obsessively buy albums, and many of the albums I buy are replacements for albums from childhood. Often, I'll listen to these albums once, realize that they aren't very good, and then shelve them, never to play them again. What I'm doing is piecing back together my childhood before it became fragmented from so many moves across the country. I hate the idea that I was careless with my childhood possessions. Doubtless, I'm making amends for my recklessness.

Other albums I buy are those I had wanted to own when I was a child but, for one reason or another, never bought. In the past five years, I have bought all of the Ohio Players's albums and David Bowie's *Pin Ups*, but when I bought a copy of Roxy Music's *Country Life*, the women on the cover weren't there. All that remained was a fern. Apparently, the cover had been censored for later pressings of the album.

I am no longer titillated by album covers that feature naked women. Ironically, the censored cover of *Country Life* is just as compelling and unsettling as the original cover that I had studiously examined as a child. The illuminated fern is cryptic, bizarre, ominous. Without the two women, all that remains is insignificant, joyless, and confusing. This is my fear of getting old: my brain playing tricks on me, urging me to remember. As soon as I conjure the two women fully in my head, they briefly materialize on the cover, but then I can no longer remember which one is doing what, so the two women fade, along with so many other people and things, from my life, diminishing until all that is left is the here and now: me, the record store, and the other men— it's almost always men—who drift in and out. We want something, but what? Some days I'm happy just to hold a stack of albums in my hands, sit on the couch in the record store, and slowly flip through them, one by one, as though looking through a photo album of old friends. Even better if a dog is sitting next to me, waiting for my fingers to rub its knobby head. Most days, I feel a yearning as bottomless as when my mother broke that Bobby Darin record, but I can't quite put my finger on what's missing, and I wonder how deep the hole is that I'll fall into should I keep looking for that thing I can't name.

LOVE TO LOVE YOU BABY

Here's the distasteful and unseemly fact of my youth: I was, from as far back as I remember, an extraordinarily randy child. Of course, there were the obvious things that excited me: any woman's boobs, bikinis, actresses on TV, hippie girls, the section of J. C. Penney that sold bras and panties, neighborhood girls, their bare legs, their butts, cutoff jeans with fringe, a girl's belly button (oh, God, the belly button!), their toes . . . all of this was part of the sexual stew bubbling inside my tiny brain, all of it tangled together, none of it quite making sense even as it so obviously affected me.

But then, of course, there were the things I kept to myself, the unusual things, the taboo things. Zira, the female chimpanzee in *Planet of the Apes*, aroused me. When Charlton Heston kissed her good-bye, I expected some man-on-monkey action to take place and was disappointed when it didn't. Nigel Olsson, Elton John's drummer, who had unusually long hair even in the 1970s, also turned my crank—that is, until I realized that Nigel was a man. What the hell kind of name was Nigel, anyway? I sure as hell didn't know anyone named Nigel in Burbank, Illinois!

How could I not have been a child deranged by horniness? Sex was everywhere. For years, my parents had been taking me to the Sheridan Drive-In at the corner of Seventy-Ninth and Harlem. The second movie was usually a women-in-prison film or a biker movie or something else that showed a lot of naked women doing things I couldn't have conjured on my own, like two women giving each other sponge baths. Did women really do that? I guessed so! My parents always assumed I was sound asleep by the time the second movie started up, but I only pretended to be asleep, shutting my eyes and lightly snoring whenever they turned around to check on me. In truth, the whole point of going to the movies was to watch the second movie. Even if we weren't actually at the drive-in, it was possible to catch an eyeful of glorious nakedness from the nearby Kmart parking lot. Whenever I went with my mother on a late-night shopping mission, I would stare at the enormous drive-in movie screen across the street, hoping to see a naked woman, and more often than not, like an answer to a prayer, a naked woman would appear.

Better than my imagination, better than images on an enormous screen, were actual naked women. Occasionally, if I kept my eyes open and stayed alert, I would get to see some forbidden flesh. For a few years during the hundreds of weekends in the 1970s I sold crap at flea markets with my father, we attracted hippie girls to our table with one of our bestselling items: a pewter ring with a marijuana leaf design made out of turquoise chips. These hippie girls were almost always braless and wore loose-fitting tops, and I would sit in such a way that I could see down their tops when they bent over to look at the rings. Did I moan out loud? Probably. Sometimes the girl would peek up, see where I was looking, and smile. Jesus, I thought, unable to look away. *Jesus*. I could have levitated tables with my boner. I could have picked up better TV reception. There was no modesty back then, no self-consciousness. The body was beautiful! The body was to be celebrated! The 1970s was like week-old bread to the 1960s: a little stiff but still good, more or less the same thing, except that it wasn't going to last as long, and you could taste its desperate decline.

There were bikers too at the flea market, and the way you could tell the difference between the hippies and bikers was that the biker guys tended to be fat whereas you rarely saw a fat hippie. Since I was fat, I thought maybe I would become a biker. Where the hippies gave off a sexual vibe, the bikers practically engaged in sex right there in front of you. Once, while at a city festival where my father and I were selling our turquoise rings, a biker guy and his girlfriend approached the table. He was fat and bearded. She was wearing very short cut-off blue jeans, the shortest cutoffs I had ever seen, and a tight black T-shirt. The fat biker bought his girlfriend one of the marijuana leaf rings for five dollars, and as they left the table, he grabbed her butt, then reached between her legs and started rubbing her crotch. She didn't stop him. In fact, she threw her head back, and her knees buckled a little. Right there, in public! For the rest of the week, I couldn't concentrate. I kept putting myself in the fat biker's place, my girlfriend's knees buckling as I touched the place I most wanted to touch. Oh, man! To be a fat biker! Forget about becoming a doctor or a lawyer or a fireman or an astronaut. I had never seen any of *them* brazenly rub a girl between her legs! If someone had asked me that week what I wanted to be when I grew up, I'd have pointed to the fat, bearded man rubbing his girlfriend's private parts in public. That's what I want to be. That man right there!

•

At a certain point, all I wanted in life was to see a photo of a vagina. Was that asking for so much?

This was all I thought about. It consumed my days and nights. In the fifth grade, my desire finally came to fruition. I found a catalog for pornographic material. My desire had been so intense, it was as though I had willed the catalog into existence. Our family lived in a condominium, and the catalog was resting in the foyer near the mailboxes. In truth, I didn't find it; I stole it. It was addressed to someone who lived in the condominium, but the catalog was too large to fit inside the tiny mailbox. But, sweet Jesus, how could I not steal it? It was like stepping outside and finding Noah's ark in your driveway. Throw a tarp over that baby and tow it inside the garage! Am I right?

The catalog was full of advertisements for explicit magazines that promised glossy photos of the most intimate variety, and for each advertised magazine, there were photos to preview what the magazine would deliver. I tucked the purloined catalog under my shirt and then brought it to the bathroom, where I immediately set up camp. And it was there, under the bright and unforgiving bathroom lights, that I saw my first vaginas. Many of them.

O, glorious vaginas!

But then I squinted. I moved the catalog closer to my face. As it turned out, the photos only intensified their mysterious nature. They weren't like ears, which looked relatively the same from person to person. Each vagina had its own temperament. Some looked shy and reserved while others looked exuberant, as though yelling something inviting out to me, like, "Hey, you! Yeah, you! Want to join me for a burger and a shake?" Others looked sad, maybe even depressed. O, melancholy vagina, how I understand thee! The photos offered no sense of perspective, either. How large was one? How small? Where did it end and where did it begin? This was long before Google. Finding so much as an anatomically correct medical drawing of a vagina would have been difficult if not impossible for a boy in the 1970s. Today, if you Google "vagina," you will get over forty-eight million results, including a news article with the headline, "Teenage Girl Arrested with Loaded Gun Hidden in Her Vagina." Back then, I had to rely on boys my own age or slightly older, and every once in a while, if I was lucky, someone would offer information, and I would be grateful, even if the information was wrong, like, "That's the hole a girl poops out of." The vagina, such as it was, was the great detective story of my youth: as elusive as the Loch Ness monster, as rare in actual eyewitness accounts as Sasquatch.

In some instances, I couldn't even see the vagina in the photos because of the thick thatch of hair surrounding it. I had yet to grow hair under my arms let alone anywhere else on my body except for the top of my head, so I was doubly fascinated by the amount of hair that grew between some of these women's legs. On those rare and startling times that I had seen my father naked, I saw hair between his legs, but since I had never seen a naked woman, I had assumed that the space between their legs, like their underarms, would be smooth. But I was mistaken.

And since this was the 1970s, when everyone looked like a tapped-out Chia Pet, I couldn't have been more wrong.

Now that I had seen photos of vaginas—many photos, in fact—I had a new goal. To touch one. There was only one obstacle, as I saw it. I was fat. And unlike fat bikers, fat boys were way, way down on the list of people who would have an opportunity to touch a girl's vagina. To my credit, I was not the fattest kid in my grade. I was the second fattest. Which meant that I was the second slowest kid running the fifty-yard dash, the second to last to get picked for a team. I comforted myself with the knowledge that I wouldn't be the last boy standing in the proverbial vagina line, waiting for his touch. That honor would go to another boy, a boy so lethargic and dull, the world slowed on its axis when you were in his presence. Also in my favor was that, unlike the fattest boy, I was a clean fat kid. And I smelled good. And I was funny. I had hoped all of these fine attributes would push me up a few more rungs, ahead of boys who stunk and were dumb. I mean, wouldn't it have been better to engage in whatever it was I was hoping to engage in with a fat boy who was clean and could make you laugh than a stinky moron who was skinny?

You would think so, but you would be wrong.

•

My knowledge of sex continued to broaden. For a short time, my father, who was always looking for an angle to make money, sold pornographic paraphernalia to the union roofers he worked with. Each morning he would load up a fake-leather case full of Super 8 movies and x-rated gag gifts. One of the gag gifts was a passport, and when you opened it, there was a naked man inside with a pop-up penis. The penis was three times as long as the man, and it sprang out of the card like a missile. If you held the passport too close to your face and opened it quickly, you'd risk poking out your own eye with the guy's cardboard dong.

The Super 8 movies were produced by a company called Swedish Erotica. Each movie came with a color booklet, and on each page of the booklet was a description of a movie accompanied by an action photo. The photos, graphic and uncensored, showed combinations of men and women the likes of which I had imagined but had never actually before seen (three women and a man; two women; two men and a woman), and the scenarios described in the plot synopses lodged themselves in my brain for years to come. But the hero of nearly every scenario was none other than a young John Holmes. Three high school cheerleaders stay after school to bone up on their sex education exam with the help of their teacher, Mr. Johnny Holmes. A lonely housewife orders a pizza, and Mr. Johnny Holmes delivers the twelve-incher himself to the famished wife. While home alone, a woman's sink springs a leak, and plumbing expert Johnny Holmes shows up with the necessary pipe. With the discovery of the Swedish Erotica movies, my sexual ambitions skyrocketed from fondling to holding a naked woman upside down, which was what Johnny Holmes was doing in one of the photos. Perhaps more startling than the sex act itself was that there was a parrot in a cage in the background. That one photo, populated with lush ferns and shag carpeting, was the epitome of 1970s decadence. It was, in short, everything I wanted to embrace for myself: a girlfriend who would let me hold her upside down during a sexual act, floor-to-ceiling mirrors surrounding the bi-level living room, a parrot in a cage. I was eleven years old when I saw that photo, and my life has never been quite the same since.

My father kept the Swedish Erotica movies in the cabinet of an old upright Brunswick phonograph that played only 78s. He kept the gag gifts in the leather case in a closet. Whenever my parents were gone, I would seek out the films that sat atop Andrew Sisters or Bing Crosby records, and then I'd watch one on our Super 8 projector. This marked the first time I saw sex. Actual sex! As weird and intimidating as it was, sex was also everything I had hoped it might be, taking place in classrooms and inside cars and near swimming pools. There were sometimes two or three women for one man. From now on, I would never be able to look at the world the same way. These movies confirmed what I had already suspected—that everywhere I went, sex had either just taken place or was about to take place. The condominium in which I had lived my until then boring as shit life was likely a hotbed of trysts, and all I needed to do was keep my eyes peeled and an ear pressed up against a wall or door. Watching those movies on the sly in my bedroom, I probably looked like some kind of bald chimpanzee, sitting on the floor and grunting with excitement as each thin story unfolded.

In eighth grade, I talked my father into financing a Magnavox VHS recorder, the price of which, with interest, was close to fifteen hundred dollars. I would pay it off over a number of years with my dog walking money. And so would begin my lifetime of debt. A blank videotape cost twenty-five dollars. A movie, like *M*A*S*H*, cost sixty dollars. One day, a copy of the movie *Inside Desiree Cousteau* appeared in our condo. My father watched it, but I was banned from watching it. I was, of course, indignant since it was my VCR being used to watch a porno. The fee for using my VCR should have been to allow me to watch any porno that appeared in our residence in VHS format.

Instead, I stayed in my bedroom and sulked, but the next time everyone was gone, I ransacked the condo. No one was going to hide a porno from me, dammit! There were only so many hiding places, and I eventually found the video. Together, my dog Shoo Shoo and I watched the movie on my VCR.

It was the first feature-length x-rated movie I had ever watched. The plot was pretty simple: As porn star Desiree Cousteau is being interviewed about her life in the adult film industry, we are privy to pornographic clips from her other movies, but then (surprise!) the interview itself turns into a porno. The movie was, in other words, a meta-porno. *Inside Desiree Cousteau* ushered in a whole era of postmodern pornos in which the stars played themselves and in which the innocent construct surrounding the pornography becomes the pornography. Not that I knew what postmodernism was. I was twelve years old. My primary goals were not to drool all over my shirt or get caught with my pants down—goals to which I still aspire.

One night, while watching the video at midnight with the volume all the way down, I heard my parents' bedroom door creak open. I quickly fumbled with the remote and turned it off, but I was sitting suspiciously close to the TV, and the remote, which was connected to the VCR by a long wire, had a two-second delay. Behind me, I heard my mother's voice.

"What are you watching, Johnny?"

I didn't have a prepared answered. I mumbled something incoherent about the Three Stooges and a tape that wasn't working.

"You're not watching that disgusting movie your father brought home, are you?"

"What movie?" I asked. "Oh, you mean . . . no, no. I'm watching the Three Stooges."

"Are you sure?" my mother asked.

Naturally, I became indignant. "Of course! I mean, I let Dad use my VCR so that he could watch it, but I can't even watch the Three Stooges now? Is that what you're saying?"

"Take it easy, Johnny. I'm just asking."

"Okay then," I said. "All right."

My mother returned to the bedroom. Of course she knew what I had been watching, but I convinced myself that I had sidestepped a disaster. All she needed to have done was walk over and ask to see the tape, and the game would have been up. *Les jeux sont fait*, as the French say. Did I rewind the tape and return it to its hiding place? No. I watched more of it once I had determined that my mother had probably fallen back to sleep. I had crossed some line. I could sense it. Shoo Shoo, a cockapoo that was smarter than many people I've met, could probably sense it, too.

All of this is to say that I was in a constant state of arousal that began around three years old, intensified throughout grade school, and culminated to a frenzy in high school. I lived in a constant state of stimulated agitation. Something had to give. I knew that much.

•

Something did give, although it took great effort on my part. At the beginning of seventh grade, I stood on the scales, saw that I had far surpassed the two-hundred-pound mark, and almost fell off of the scales, dizzy as I was with the realization that I was fatter than I had imagined possible. That was when my early jogs in the fields behind the condos began, as well as my diet. By high school, I was thin. I had lost ninety pounds, so it was possible that I was too thin, but I wasn't complaining. I had also gained some height, which stretched me even more, narrowing my waist to twenty-eight inches.

My transformation frightened my grade school classmates, some of whom seemed angry at me, as though my newfound skinniness was a betrayal of their already cemented opinion that I was fat, but to the girls in high school who had come from other schools, I had never been fat. This was the great illusion that I had created. For the first time since kindergarten, girls paid attention to me, some even pursued me, and while I didn't outright reject their advances, I also didn't take advantage of them. For a boy whose primary goal in life was to touch a girl's vagina, this created an excruciating kind of pain.

At the annual Illinois Drama Festival my freshman year, while staying in a hotel with hundreds of other horny high school students across the state, Lydia, who was two years older, asked me to spend the night in bed with her.

"Are you okay with that?" she asked.

Was this a trick question?

I smiled. I nodded. My voice was changing, so I avoided speaking, fearing a sudden high-pitched crack in my voice would ruin the mood.

Until then, I had never met a girl as sexually overt as Lydia. Every day at lunch, she talked about sex. Eight of us sat at a round table

while Lydia held forth on subjects as wide-ranging as orgies and mastur-
bation. I would sit quietly, eating my rubbery slice of pizza and sipping
my watery milkshake, paying close attention. Every word that came out
of Lydia's mouth conjured naughty images. She claimed to have had
older lovers—men, not boys—and she claimed to have been friends with
numerous gay boys from other schools. To the best of my knowledge, I
had never even met anyone who was gay, let alone been friends with a gay
person. (Years later, as several former classmates came out of the closet,
I would come to realize that I was one of the few straight boys, if not the
only straight boy, in Drama Club.) During lunch, Lydia would say (loud
enough for everyone to hear), "You're always welcome in my bed, John"
or "When you decide you want to lose your virginity, just let me know."

And now—fourteen years old, away from home for the first time,
and staying in a hotel room in a city named Normal, of all places—I
was going to lose my virginity. We left the party where we had been
playing obscene Mad Libs and walked back to her room. She was
already wearing her clothes for bed—sweatpants and a tight T-shirt—
as was I—a polyester tracksuit that my mother had bought me at Sears
Outlet. The tracksuit had matching pants and a zip-up top, and the
fabric felt like sponge. Lydia and I slipped into bed, we snuggled, and
I was ready to kiss her, but she said, "The room's spinning." Lydia had
been drinking whiskey. I'd had a few sips of beer, nothing more. "Oh,"
I said, my boner creating a pup tent in my pants. "Hold me," Lydia
said, and then she faced away from me. I pressed myself against her,
my hard-on pressed against her butt, and I draped an arm around her.
I couldn't sleep, though. My boner thumped repeatedly against Lydia,
like the walking stick of an old man knocking at a locked door: "Hello?
Anybody there? Hello? Would someone please open up? It's Hyram
Braxton, dammit! Let me in!"

Each time someone opened up the door to our room and poked
their head inside, I pretended I was asleep. The reaction was same each
time: Holy shit, John and Lydia hooked up! This was a rumor I wasn't

going to deny. After all, I was a boy who really wanted to have sex. And when we returned to school, the rumor circulated.

"So, you like older women?" a girl asked me by my locker between classes. I didn't even know her, but my reputation preceded me.

"Yeah. I guess," I said. "I don't know. Sure. I suppose." I blushed. (I have rosacea; I blush easily.)

"Sweet," she said, touching my feverish cheek and moving along.

•

With total objectivity and without any ego, I can now say that during my four years of high school I was a pretty good-looking kid. I can say this because shortly after high school I started losing my hair and gaining weight again, and for the rest of my time on this planet (which, granted, isn't yet over but which is nonetheless much closer to the end than it is to the beginning), I never regained those good looks again. They came and went, like a fart in a large auditorium. I knew for that short time what it was like to be pined for by women I didn't know based purely on physical appearance. It was exhilarating but ultimately confusing—confusing because I had been a fat boy for so long, a fat boy who certainly hadn't inspired lust.

I may not have taken fullest advantage of the lust I inspired, but I didn't push it away. Freshman year, Kathy Urbanski sat on my lap during the last half of geometry class, grinding into my groin, while the teacher ignored us. Kathy was dating a senior who wore a black leather jacket like Sylvester Stallone in *The Lords of Flatbush*, and each day Kathy would whisper into my ear, "Don't tell Jimmy about this, okay?" Why the hell would I tell Jimmy? Did I want Jimmy and his hooligan friends to jump me after school, shoving my face into the concrete, because his girlfriend wanted to give me a lap dance during geometry, a class I would eventually fail, unable to concentrate thanks to Kathy Urbanski and my unflagging sexual cravings?

That fall, during a weekend theater tournament, a girl from another school openly flirted with me. She had strawberry blond hair, and we kept crossing paths in the long, cavernous, darkened hallways. I still remember the weather, how it was one of those first truly cusp-of-winter days that's so typical of Chicago: pleasantly cool and breezy with gray clouds churning overhead. Most of the school was lit by whatever light filtered in from outside, and that wasn't much. The girl and I would accidentally run into each other in the hall, and each time this happened she would interrogate me: What year was I? Did I have a girlfriend? Had anyone ever told me I was cute? By then, I had read enough *Penthouse* letters that I started to construct one in my head: *Dear Penthouse Forum: It was supposed to have been a typical drama tournament at my high school, but all of that changed when the girl with strawberry blond hair told me to meet her on the catwalk backstage. Slowly, I climbed the ladder. I wasn't even sure she would be there. But lo and behold, there she was, resting on a pile of the stage crew's muslin, naked and with her legs spread, rubbing herself while softly singing the opening lines of* Annie's *theme song. Believe you me, the sun wasn't the only thing that was gonna come up!* But of course nothing happened. We didn't even kiss. She mock-pouted when she walked back to her bus. I sometimes wonder if I had dreamed her. I sometimes wonder if I have dreamed all of the girls who drove me into a state of hallucinatory frenzy.

In my French class one day, I overheard a girl named Christine talk about her boyfriend's penis. "It gets about this long and really, really purple, but what I love is that it gets that way because of me."

Purple? I thought. And how far apart did she hold her hands?

That same day, I went to the chalkboard and accidentally wrote the French word for *pubic* instead of *public*. My French teacher gave me a wicked look and said, "*O la la, monsieur!*"

After a speech tournament in which I had failed to win any prize for my one-man comedic role, I flirted with Jennifer Brown on the long bus ride back home. When it was just the two of us remaining, along with the bus driver, I kissed Jennifer and ran my hand up her thigh. She was wearing a skirt, and I could feel the edge of her underwear. And heat. "Go ahead," she said. "Touch me."

But I didn't. I couldn't. I must have known that once I touched her there, it would mean more than the act itself. Intuitively, I knew that I would be engaging in an unspoken contract that would require movie dates and time spent together, and, Christ, maybe marriage and babies and other stuff I wasn't ready for. I liked Jennifer—I did—but I wasn't ready for what touching her between her legs implied. The looming shadow of implications may not have been as grandiose as the touching of forefingers in Michelangelo's *The Creation of Adam*, but on that dark bus, lying side by side on the hard green seat, it certainly felt about as biblical and burdensome as the beginning of mankind.

•

I also, much to my own bewilderment, attracted the attention of both boys and men. A boy in my dramatic arts class—a boy who, in the fourth grade, I had hit over the head with a hard plastic ruler for poking me in the spine—stared dreamily at me from across the aisle.

"Stop it," I would say under my breath, but the more I told him to stop staring at me that way, the more exaggerated his puppy dog looks became.

And then there was my French teacher, whom we called Monsieur. As the only advanced French student in my entire school, I was required to spend extra time with him during my homeroom hour. After I took a seat, Monsieur would squeeze himself into a too-small student desk and then scoot it close to me. It's obvious to me now that Monsieur was gay, although, as I noted earlier, I didn't at the time think anyone I knew was gay. Burbank was a working-class neighborhood, sheltered, often in denial. A gay teacher? Puh-*lease*. And yet he *was* gay, as were other teachers, I now realize. Whenever we took a French club field trip, Monsieur would disappear for the entire day while we wandered downtown Chicago on our own. When he met us at the bus at the end of the day—disheveled, possibly drunk—the girls in the class would tease him.

"Did you have a hot date?" they would ask, and he would grin mischievously and blush.

What *had* he been doing all day? I now have suspicions that I didn't have then.

One day, Monsieur pulled his desk next to mine, until we were almost touching, and said, "Oh, you won't believe the morning I had. When I got out of the shower, I started putting on my deodorant when the roller ball fell out, and all the deodorant dripped down my naked body." He was staring into my eyes when he said "my naked body," and I looked away. His leg was touching my leg. His knuckles, which rested on my desk, were extraordinarily hairy, like Lon Chaney Jr.'s knuckles in *The Wolfman* when he's in the process of transforming into the hirsute monster.

I never returned for another special session. I wasn't angry with him. I just felt uncomfortable. At the time, I couldn't articulate why I felt uncomfortable, so I would make up excuses for why I couldn't be there. *I have to work on yearbook. I have to work on the newspaper. I have a test to make up. I have to memorize my lines for a play.*

I felt no ill will toward Monsieur. Still, I told no one. It was, as the French would say, *entre nous*. Between us.

●

I knew Beckie from Drama Club, but it wasn't until the theater festival my junior year of high school that things started to heat up between us. As with Lydia two years earlier, we were staying in a motel room in Normal, Illinois, and a bunch of us were hanging out in a room one night when one of the boys said, "Okay, it's time to go to sleep." He quickly flipped off the light. It was, I realized, a ploy to keep the girls in the room. Instead of going back to my own room, I lay on top of Beckie. I weighed probably 118 pounds, so I could lie on top of a woman back then without damaging her internal organs or suffocating her.

Even in this position, with my boner acting as a crowbar, trying to pry its way out of my sweatpants, I was too shy to make the move. But Beckie wasn't. She kissed me. And kept kissing me. With the room full of partnered and unpartnered classmates, possibly even another couple in the same bed (I no longer remember), we didn't do anything more than kiss, but we kissed all night. The next day's joke between us was how we needed toothpicks to keep our eyes open.

But didn't Beckie have a boyfriend? And wasn't he some mystery man from another school?

Once we returned home from Normal—my own Xanadu where I was now two-for-two in the spending-the-night-in-the-same-bed-with-a-girl department—I decided not to pursue Beckie because of her status as a taken woman. I did, however, ceaselessly draw adoring caricatures of her that I would fold into a paper football and, using my forefinger, punt toward her. Since my parents had moved us from the condominium to a house, I now had my own bedroom—and a private one, at that, situated on the second floor—and so Beckie and I began to have study sessions together. My mother trusted me enough to let me take Beckie to my bedroom for these sessions, although occasionally she would yell up the stairs to ask if we needed anything. "Would your friend like something to drink? Would your friend like some popcorn? Would your friend like a Sloppy Joe?" "No! No! No! We're fine!" I used these study opportunities to impress Beckie with my deep appreciation of old movies and contemporary music. Instead of seizing these times together as openings to kiss her, I treated her to elaborate show and tell sessions.

"Look. This is an actual script from an Abbott and Costello movie. Look. Here's an original movie poster from *Abbott and Costello Meet the Killer, Boris Karloff*. Boris Karloff isn't even the killer. He just had a contractual agreement that his name should be in the title. How weird is that! The poster is called a one-sheet, by the way. Look. Here's the rare British pressing of Elton John's first album, *Empty Sky*."

I filled the air with meaningless and stultifying trivia. It's a wonder she didn't jump out my bedroom's second floor window. Did we eventually kiss? Yes. Did I initiate it? No. I no longer remember the circumstances, although it was probably somewhere between me saying, "Look! Here's my *Planet of the Apes* Dr. Zaius bank!" and "Look! A deck of Jimmy Stewart playing cards, circa 1956!" This was the only time in my life my hair ever looked good, and I would never again be as thin as I was that year, and I was occasionally funny when I wasn't moody, but I was not smooth. I had no game. I had decided that "our song" would be Little River Band's "Take It Easy on Me." That's how much game I had. That's how smooth.

It was April. Spring. Shortly after it was determined that Beckie had officially broken up with her mystery man and that we were officially to be boyfriend and girlfriend, two things happened that nearly derailed our momentum. A massive amount of snow got dumped on Chicago, crushing spring like an ant underfoot. And then I got sick. Really sick. I missed a week of school. I could barely move. Beckie, however, was not sick. She was out there in the world, able to associate freely with any number of men, both known and unknown to me.

But she didn't. She called every day. She told me she had a surprise for me. She set a date for the surprise.

"What is it?"

"Can't you guess, silly?" she replied.

No, I couldn't. Was it something to do with Abbott and Costello? Or Elton John? Or *Planet of the Apes*?

"But only if you're better," she said. "I wouldn't want to make you worse."

"What kind of a gift would make me worse?" I asked.

I waited. I willed myself to get better. I stared at the snow, hoping to melt it with the sheer force of my concentration. A week later, Beckie came to my house, and I quickly escorted her upstairs. We kissed. And kissed. It had been a long time since I'd seen her. My goal—the goal that continued to elude me—was no longer on my mind. I simply liked being with Beckie. I liked boring her to tears with my knowledge of mundane facts. I liked that she laughed at my jokes. I liked drawing caricatures of her. My heart sped up at the sight of her. Even though I knew deep down that all of this would come at a cost, I ignored that part of it. These were still the halcyon days of the relationship, when everything was beautiful and promising.

"Do you trust me?" she asked between kisses.

"Sure," I said. "Of course."

"I've never done anything like this before."

"Like what?"

And then she slipped her hand down my pants, underneath the elastic band of my underwear, until she reached what she wanted to reach.

"Is that a bone?" she asked, squeezing it.

"Sort of," I said.

I unfastened and unzipped my pants. I showed her what she was touching.

"Oh," she said once I had freed myself. "Here," she said, letting go of me so that she could unbuckle and unzip her own pants. And then she took hold of my hand, leading it toward its destination. Holy shit! Was this really happening? After all these painful years of imagining it? After so many close calls? Was this going to be the moment?

She placed my hand into her pants, under the elastic of her underwear, and then, on my own, I reached farther. And farther. And farther. Until . . .

Sweet Jesus!

•

You may be disappointed that my story doesn't end in a shag-carpeted room with a parrot in a cage, but there would be many years ahead of me for those hijinks. As for the boy who really, really wanted to have sex, he had set out looking for one thing but found something else instead.

He found love. And then, four months later, he found heartache. He probably should have stuck to his main objective, but he couldn't keep his eye on the ball. He strayed. And look what happened. And, oh, how it hurt. The poor bastard. The poor son of a bitch.

But what a glorious world where a fat little boy can achieve his goals. What a lovely and complicated life, even when the still-beating heart is torn in two.

THE FAT BOY
CODA

AFTER THE FAT

What happens to the fat boy when he grows up?

Well: he gets two graduate degrees; he writes books; he gets married and divorced not once but twice; he gains weight and loses weight and then gains it back and then loses it again (and then gains it back); for twenty years he starts every morning by eating a banana and drinking an ice-cold Frappuccino in a bottle; he has had too many dogs and cats to count, but as he types this he has four cats, one of them blind and so old she has to be carried to her food because she easily becomes disoriented, walking in an endless tight circle until a hand reaches down and gently stops her; after he turns fifty, he gets four tattoos with plans to get more; he has a bum knee, a weak ankle, and a shoulder that aches most days and nights; he sometimes has a girlfriend and sometimes doesn't; he is nomadic, having lived all over the country, including ten states and the District of Columbia, and often itching to be somewhere other than where he is; he spends more and more time alone, but he's not sure why; he is restless; he works too much; or maybe he's lazy (he's never sure which it is); after years as a fat boy wondering where girls hang out, he meets them everywhere now; he meets them at wine tastings, at karaoke, at conferences, at bars, at restaurants, at a place called the Chicken Hut, at parties, at work, at literary readings, near jukeboxes, on trains, online, on rooftops, in hotel bars, in hotel lobbies, even, once, in a closet; he has learned that the art of looking is not to look; he has learned that the least attractive quality is desperation; he has learned that most lost things can be found by looking under things; he is a creature of habit; he is not without regrets; he is sometimes reckless; he wants chiseled on his headstone, *He knew better but did it anyway*; or maybe, simply, *His animals loved him*. But this is a lie. He doesn't want to be buried, doesn't want a headstone. He wants to be a box of ashes, but hopefully not anytime soon.

I'm fifty-one years old now. Almost fifty-two. Most days I keep myself in check by sitting in a chair and listening to an album. Every once in a while, if the sunlight streaming into my house hits the floor a certain way or if the room suddenly shifts from light to dark because of the movement of clouds, this combination of song that's playing on the turntable and mood that's created by the natural light will transport me back to the moment when I first heard the song or to a time when that song played persistently in the background, and I can feel the warmth behind my eyes, my vision growing blurry, not because of a specific memory or out of sentimentality but because of a vague feeling of all that's happened between then and now, because of all that's been lost. This emotion hits me unexpectedly, forcefully, and then it leaves no sooner than it arrived, before I can even process what just happened. The past is like a magician's flash paper, a surprising burst of flame that comes and goes before you fully understand what's happened. The only way to harness it is to write it down, quickly, before it leaves and never comes back.

Many of the people I've written about are gone now. My mother died in a hospital in 1988. I was by her side. She was fifty-four. When she took her last breath, after it was obvious that there would be no more, I thought, All those stories . . . gone. And then the grief at losing this woman in whom I had confided so much took root deep inside me where it would remain for several months until one afternoon, back home and sleeping on the couch, I had a dream that she took hold of my hand and said, I'm okay. Everything's okay. And then the grief lifted.

My father died nearly twenty-five years later, in 2013, in a hospital emergency room. He was eighty. I didn't cry upon hearing the news. It bothers me that I haven't had the expected emotional response at the news, but I didn't then and haven't since. As he got older, he became more combative. The last few times I visited him, I couldn't even stay in his house for longer than a few minutes. He had become a hoarder, and his dogs weren't housebroken. After only a few seconds inside, my eyes would start to burn.

I drove 675 miles to his memorial service in Poplar Bluff, Missouri, and since I hadn't prepared to speak but was expected to say a few words, I walked to the podium and talked off the cuff about what a hardheaded man he was. A hard worker, to be sure, and someone who instilled a strong work ethic in me, but, Jesus Christ, what a hard head that man had! I even offered up a few examples as solid and irrefutable evidence. I expected a few laughs because anyone who knew my father knew that I was speaking the truth, that Bob McNally was one stubborn SOB, often to his own detriment, but no one smiled. My father would have appreciated my honesty at least.

The next morning, I headed back to North Carolina, disappointed by the sentimentality of the service. In truth, I couldn't get out of that town fast enough. I wanted to leave it all behind, and leave it behind I did.

So many people from my past may be gone, but there are still those tangible things that can be replaced. These days my compulsion leads me to garage sales and thrift stores, to online marketplaces and the basements of people I barely know. Instead of buying the newest computer or the latest wireless stereo receiver, I search for vintage typewriters and turntables. The line between collector and hoarder can be a thin one sometimes, and I'm always mindful of staying on the side of the former. If I can afford it, I replace the things I've lost, but sometimes the cost is too great, and I have no choice. I let it go.

In recent years I've bought a half-dozen sets of speakers from the sixties and seventies, 8-track and cassette decks, a Zenith stereo console. I've bought old movie projectors. I own two Kodak carousel slide projectors from two different decades. I plan to buy boxes of vacation slides for my projector. They sell them on eBay—whole boxes of slides from strangers' vacations. I can load them into a projector, illuminate them on a wall, and imagine what another childhood might have been like.

But I don't live in the past; I'm eager to see what's next in store for me. When collecting relics from my childhood, I tell myself that everyone needs a hobby, and this one is mine. I get especially excited when I find something from my past that had gone missing or was damaged and had to be thrown away. I'm sure there's a deeper psychological reason for doing this—I'm sure it goes back to our family losing everything in the mobile home fire—but I don't dwell on it.

•

I don't dwell. And yet I sometimes can't help imagining an alternative universe, one where Aunt Peggy didn't force-feed me while my mother was in the hospital, igniting my constant hunger; one where Beckie never noticed that dime-sized spot on the crown of my head. Perhaps if the spot had gone unnoticed, it never would have gained the confidence to spread. I suspect the baldness didn't start on that seemingly fateful day, that it began years earlier with a flickering premonition. When I look back at my kindergarten photo of that stone-faced boy with the big ears, I can't help but wonder if I was having a vision that morning, a vision not of love lost or of financial ruin, as I'd once thought, but of hair, *my* hair. Had I already seen its future—or, rather, its grim lack thereof? It's hard to believe that I wasn't seeing something that would later test my mettle. When I stare into that little boy's eyes, I don't envy him much, certainly not the next several years of his life, but I do envy him his hair—every last shimmering strand.

ACKNOWLEDGMENTS

My gratitude to the editors who published earlier versions of these chapters in the following magazines: "Courting Disaster" in *Moon City Review*; "The Genius and I" and "The Kindergarten of Earthly Delights" in *Booth*; "Working Stiff" in the anthology *We Speak Chicagoese*; "In the Field behind the Condo Where the Fat Boy Plays" in the *Common*; "The Coward" (under the title "The World, and the Difficulty of Living in It") in *Criminal Class Review*; "On Being a Lazy Fuck" in *Chicago Literati*; "Sweet Bionic Jesus" in *Hypertext Review*; "Picture Day" (under the title "Hair Today . . .") in the anthology *When I Was a Loser*. My thanks, in particular, to Jennifer Murvin, Robert Stapleton, Dennis Foley, James Alan Gill, Kevin Whiteley, Abby Sheaffer, and Christine Maul Rice.

My gratitude also to the following good people:

Bill Hillmann, who got the ball rolling by introducing me to Jacob Knabb.

Jacob Knabb, who showed early support for the book and has become a friend, for which I'm grateful.

Shelley Washburn, director of Pacific University's low-residency MFA program, for inviting me to be on the program's faculty. It was in the sleepy Oregon towns of Seaside and Forest Grove where I first tried out many of these chapters, reading them aloud to students and faculty. Everyone's kindness served as fuel for me to continue working on this book.

The faculty at Pacific University, whose company I'm always honored to be among.

The students at Pacific University, whose enthusiasm each residency reminds me why I write: joy.

My permanent teaching home, the University of Louisiana at Lafayette, where I have a schedule that allows me to work on several projects at once and still have time to buy used records in bulk.

Dayana Stetco, friend and department head, for her support in these endeavors.

Drew Attana, who read an earlier version of this manuscript and offered his thoughtful feedback. Thanks, man.

Krista Marie DeBehnke for, along with Drew, helping out with my animals these past few years. Thank you for your friendship.

Dan Prazer, old friend, who, via serendipity, has found himself helping out with this book's production. I'm in good hands.

The extraordinarily talented designer Amanda Schwarz who, in coming up with cover designs, provided an embarrassment of riches to choose from.

The all-star Elephant Rock Books team: Anne McPeak, Christopher Morris, Kathryn Fitzpatrick, and Chloe Spinnanger.

Jotham Burrello, publisher of Elephant Rock Books, whose friendship I value and for whose investment in this slice of my life I am grateful.

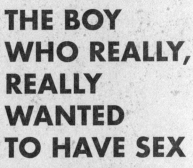

THE BOY WHO REALLY, REALLY WANTED TO HAVE SEX

THE MEMOIR OF A FAT KID

JOHN McNALLY

ELEPHANT ROCK BOOKS

Ashford : Connecticut
elephantrockbooks.com

ERB publisher Jotham Burrello discusses the writing of the memoir with author John McNally.

Jotham Burrello: If a genie granted you a wish to go back to any episode in the memoir, what would it be? And what would you do differently?

John McNally: To be honest, there isn't a specific moment I would want to relive. If I could, I'd try to talk my mother into quitting smoking. She died at fifty-four from cancer. She was a good person, and I wish I'd had more time with her, so maybe that three-year-old who runs inside the trailer to fetch his mother her cigarettes might instead concoct a scheme to make her stop smoking. Are there things I wish I'd done differently as a child? Sure. Would I want to go back and do things differently? No.

JB: The memoir evolved over the years as you published individual essays of your childhood. When did you start to examine your childhood through this reflective lens?

JM: Probably in childhood!

JB: Seriously?

JM: Seriously. When I was a child, I always imagined the older version of myself looking back to the age I was at the time. But more to your point, I wrote most of these essays during a time of transition. In a very short period, three things happened: I got divorced, my father died, and I took a new job that was nine hundred miles away from where I had spent the previous eleven years. I was burned out writing fiction, so I began writing a few short essays about childhood, but the more I wrote, the more I remembered, and the more I remembered, the more essays I wanted to write.

JB: So you had no real guide besides your memory.

JM: Right. The essays' direction often veered off course. For instance, I would begin writing an essay about my mother only to realize, halfway through, that my father had taken over. Or I would begin to write about one subject (jobs I'd had as a child) only to find myself writing about something else (my relationship with my father). That's what was exciting. I would begin one place but end up at the unexpected. I wrote to discover the unexpected.

JB: Once you started to compose a book from these unexpected discoveries, how did you determine what to include and what to leave out?

JM: I allowed the writing to dictate those decisions. In other words, while writing one chapter, the seed of another chapter would present itself to me, and then that's the chapter I would write next.

JB: As you mentioned above, curiosity and memory guided you.

JM: Exactly. I tried not to impose moments from my life onto the book, which is, I'll confess, an odd way of writing. The book is impressionistic rather than linear. And I'm normally a linear writer.

JB: And the structure, as you say in the prologue, is not framed by linear time. The construction mimics your writing process for the book.

JM: The book is also short. After the last chapter that I wrote (which isn't the last chapter in the finished book), I kept thinking that I needed to write more, but I had written everything that I wanted to write about this aspect of my life as a fat boy. Now, it's entirely possible that I'll want to write a completely different memoir later that takes place over the same period of time, and it's possible that such a book would be linear and more consciously constructed. But that book hasn't called out to me yet.

JB: Readers have told me that parts of the book are laugh-out-loud funny. All of your work has a comic element to it. Are you aware of the humor as you're writing? Do you have a favorite funny section (from your life)?

JM: I know that my worldview is filtered through a comic, sometimes absurd, sometimes darkly comic lens. But I don't try to be funny. My eye naturally wanders to the absurd. I'll tell anecdotes to friends who'll say, "Those things only happen to you, McNally," and I'll think, surely not just to me . . . but those are the things I pay attention to.

JB: Do you revise for humor?

JM: One of the things I revise for is timing. I've read much of this book aloud to an audience of students and faculty at Pacific University's MFA program, and those readings (spread out over several years) were great opportunities to hear what was working and what wasn't. I'll sometimes revise as I'm reading based on how the audience is responding. The things that I personally find funniest in my life (and in this book) are probably not the things that general public would pick out.

JB: For instance?

JM: For instance, I get a kick out of the younger me watching an adult movie with my dog, Shoo Shoo. It's absurd! There are more dignified comic moments in the book, but as I point out in the book, I'm still sometimes that little boy. And that little boy would have found that moment funny if he had read it in a book or seen it in a movie.

JB: Do you think society's attitude toward overweight people has changed since you were, well, a fat boy?

JM: Absolutely. We still have a long way to go, but, yes, it's definitely changed. I showed the mock-up covers of the book (all of which featured my childhood photos) to a friend, and she wrote back how it was funny that I was considered fat because I wouldn't have been considered fat today. She teaches high school, so I trust her opinion. But in the 1970s? I was ridiculed by adults. Not occasionally, either. Not infrequently. *Every single day.* They didn't care if I heard them say something. In fact, they often said things directly to me. Or they would call me a name as I rode my bike by. I'm sure that kind of verbal abuse still happens today, but I honestly don't see it happening with any frequency, and I think most people would be appalled by it. If I ever saw an adult say something to a kid the way adults said things to me, I would have a word with them. But as an adult I've never seen that behavior.

JB: Does your writing process differ when writing memoir versus writing fiction?

JM: Not much. Whether it's memoir or fiction, I allow the story to lead me where it needs to go. In both, the writing is led by my unconscious mind—in memoir, the fuel is memory; in fiction, the fuel is imagination. But the process is essentially the same because my goal in both is to write something that makes me wonder what it's all about, and the revision process it to solve that riddle.

JB: And how do you revise a memory?

JM: Memory is hazy; memory isn't always accurate. So, I would Google details about a shopping mall or what the weather was like in a particular month. I would ask friends about certain details to see how their memory lined up with mine. I would look at photographs. Sometimes when I transferred a photo onto the computer, I would notice things I hadn't seen before. You think you know what's in a photo you've looked at a thousand times before, but from a new perspective you realize that there's a world inside the photo you've missed. Oftentimes I looked at photos just to put myself back to that time and place. It was my way to time travel.

JB: How about use of interviews?

JM: Before my father died, I interviewed him for a book I thought I might write one day. His memory wasn't always the best record of events, but he reminded me of details I had forgotten. Revision also means omitting things that weren't necessary for a certain scene. Even if you're writing about real life, the writer's obligation is to shape it. Let's face it: a faithful rendering of life would mean writing thousands of volumes of mundane details with occasional punctuated moments. My job is to look for those moments of punctuation and bring them to life.

JB: Have you ventured into playwriting since your stint in *Chunkyobdangle?*

JM: I've taken a forty-three-year break from playwriting. But I do write screenplays and TV pilots. Lately, I've been considering writing a play. I just need the right material for the medium. It would be nice to come full circle. But I won't act in it this time. I'll leave the acting to professionals.

JB: "The Hippest Trip in Burbank" deals mainly with your experiences handling racial tensions growing up on Chicago's Southside. We both know there is a long history of racial division in the city. You say that there is no real moral to the story, but what do you think it communicates to readers?

JM: I'm not sure what it communicates to readers because I don't think about that when I'm writing. It's likely going to communicate different things to different readers. This was the most difficult chapter for me to write because I had to face some unpleasant things about the boy I was and what that means. It's easy to give yourself a pass if you're in a position to give yourself a pass. In many ways, it's a chapter about degrees of being complicit. It's also about my own nagging guilt as an adult for doing something as a child that I shouldn't have done. But I'm not sure that there's an obvious takeaway from that chapter. My hope is that it leaves an impression rather than a lesson. That impression will depend upon the reader, I suppose.

JB: Growing up your father moved the family to Houston but soon returned to Chicagoland. Now you live in North Carolina and teach in Louisiana. Do you still consider yourself a Midwesterner?

JM: I absolutely consider myself a Midwesterner. More so, I consider myself a Chicagoan. I've also lived in Southern Illinois, Nebraska, Iowa, and Wisconsin, and I can assure you that *Midwestern* is interpreted differently in each place. Generally, I'm a Midwesterner. Specifically, I'm a Chicagoan. However you want to define the Chicago sensibility, I probably embody it.

JB: As a self-diagnosed "lazy fuck," how do you motivate yourself to churn out so much work?

JM: I write just a little every day, but it adds up. That's the trick: consistency. If you can make consistency a habit, you can afford to be lazy in other aspects of your life. I used to try to write all day, but I would burn myself out, so now I write until I don't want to write anymore.

JB: Do you still own that Loch Ness monster book?

JM: I do still own the Loch Ness monster book. And I still intend to read it. One of these days.

JB: Have you kept in touch with any of these characters from your childhood? Like Jimmy Finger, for instance. Did anyone besides your parents ever find out that you two were the ones who "robbed" that house?

JM: I keep in touch with a few of the characters from my childhood, but not many. After *The Book of Ralph* came out—which is a novel about my neighborhood—I was in touch again with several people I hadn't spoken to in years. I visited my grade school and high school to give talks, so I saw some of my old teachers again, too. But by and large, no, I'm not in touch. I hear that Jimmy Finger still lives at home. As far as I know, no one else knew about our adventure at that house. Now that I think about it, I should probably look up the statute of limitations before this book goes to press.

JB: Have you committed other minor crimes?

JM: No. After my brief foray into the world of crime, I've become, from fourth grade until today, a model citizen. I live the straight and narrow. Well . . . *mostly*.

QUESTIONS FOR DISCUSSION

1. One of the epigraphs at the beginning of the memoir is from Charles Dickens's *David Copperfield*. Why do you think McNally chose this quote? What does it foretell about the story?

2. McNally opts to tell this story out of order, jumping around from event to event. Still, though, we get a strong sense of him growing out of his childhood as the story comes to an end. How does McNally change from the beginning of the memoir to the end? What one period of McNally's childhood do you feel shows a dramatic transformation?

3. McNally sometimes wonders how his life might have been different if certain things either had happened or hadn't happened. This is particularly true of the final chapter, where he says that he "sometimes can't help imagining an alternative universe, one where Aunt Peggy didn't force-feed me . . . one where Beckie never noticed that dime-sized spot on the crown of my head." He even fantasizes about loading slide shows of strangers' vacations into his projector and imagining "what another childhood might have been like." What, then, do you think McNally's attitude toward his childhood ultimately is?

4. One of the most important relationships in the memoir is the one between McNally and his childhood girlfriend Beckie. Do you think she was the reason for his future romantic problems, or do they have more to do with his own insecurities? What is it about Beckie that makes McNally's encounters with her so pivotal and formative?

5. Throughout the story, McNally details his increasingly strained relationship with his father. Why do you think McNally and his father grew so far apart, and what effects do you see that strained relationship having on McNally as the story progresses?

6. Now juxtapose McNally's relationship with his father against his relationship with his mother. What about his relationship with his mother was different, and why was it different?

7. McNally divides "The Coward" between two stories and two points of view: that of him as a boy and that of him as an adult. Why does he tell us the story of his antagonistic relationship with Vik? Why is it so important to the larger story of his childhood?

8. McNally's family moves around quite a bit, and some of those moves make his life difficult in surprising and even frightening ways. Think, for example, of his experiences at that "experimental school" in Houston. What role does setting play in this memoir, and what effect does it have on McNally's childhood?

9. Memoirs tell the story of a part of life or a seminal period in a life. Range back over your own life. What moments are memoir worthy? What characters are vital to the telling?

10. And then, of course, there's the obvious: McNally's fascination with the women and girls he meets. This hits us immediately in "Courting Disaster" and then comes up again and again in chapters like "The Kindergarten of Earthly Delights." What exactly is the nature of his fascination with the opposite sex, and what about it—if anything—changes during his encounter with Beckie in "Love to Love You Baby"?

ALSO BY ELEPHANT ROCK BOOKS

The Art of Holding On and Letting Go
by **Kristin Bartley Lenz**

"Eloquent debut."
–Booklist / Junior Library Guild Selection

The Carnival at Bray
by **Jessie Ann Foley**

"Powerfully Evocative!"
–Kirkus Reviews, Starred Review;
   Printz Honor Book & Morris Finalist

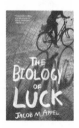

The Biology of Luck
by **Jacob M. Appel**

"Clever, vigorously written, intently observed,
   and richly emotional."
–Booklist

Briefly Knocked Unconscious by a Low-Flying Duck:
Stories from 2nd Story

"This collection will demand, and receive, return
   trips from its readers."
–Publishers Weekly, Starred Review

The Temple of Air
by **Patricia Ann McNair**

"This is a beautiful book, intense and original."
–Audrey Niffenegger